Stone & *Feather*

Stone & *Feather*

Steven Holl Architects / The Nelson-Atkins Museum Expansion

Essay by Jeffrey Kipnis
with contributions by Steven Holl and Chris McVoy

and an introductory essay by Marc F. Wilson

Principal photography by Roland Halbe

The Nelson-Atkins Museum of Art

PRESTEL MUNICH – BERLIN – LONDON – NEW YORK

Front cover and frontispiece: Views of the Bloch
(left) and Nelson-Atkins buildings reflected by the
pool in the J. C. Nichols Plaza; in the foreground,
Walter De Maria's *One Sun / 34 Moons* (2002).

Library of Congress Control Number: 2007925943
British Library Cataloguing-in-Publication Data:
a catalogue record for this book is available from
the British Library. The Deutsche Bibliothek holds
a record of this publication in the Deutsche
Nationalbibliografie; detailed bibliographical
data can be found under: *http://dnb.ddb.de*

Copyright © 2007 by the Trustees of the
Nelson Gallery Foundation
The Nelson-Atkins Museum of Art
4525 Oak Street
Kansas City, MO 64111

Copyright © 2007 Prestel Verlag,
Munich–Berlin–London–New York

Drawings © Steven Holl Architects
Watercolors © Steven Holl

Color Separations / Proofs: ReproLine Mediateam,
Munich
Printing and Binding: Passavia, Passau
Printed in Germany on acid-free paper

ISBN 978-3-7913-3803-3 (trade edition)
ISBN 978-3-7913-6143-7 (museum edition)

Prestel Verlag
Königinstrasse 9
80539 Munich
Tel. +49 (89) 38 17 09-0
Fax +49 (89) 38 17 09-35

Prestel Publishing Ltd.
4, Bloomsbury Place
London WC1A 2QA
Tel. +44 (0) 20 7323-5004
Fax +44 (0) 20 7636-8004

Prestel Publishing
900 Broadway. Suite 603
New York, N.Y. 10003
Tel. +1 (212) 995-2720
Fax +1 (212) 995-2733
www.prestel.com

Prestel books are available worldwide.
Please contact your nearest bookseller or
one of the above addresses for information
concerning your local distributor.

ILLUSTRATION CREDITS

*Unless otherwise credited below, all photographs by
Roland Halbe.*

©Steven Holl Architects: pp. 187, 191, all drawings

©Timothy Hursley: p. 13

©Erich Lessing/Art Resource: p. 31

©Mel McLean: p. 46

©Jamison Miller: pp. 22, 30

©Chris McVoy: pp. 164, 188, 189 (left), 193,
195, 200

©Jeff Nightingale: pp. 95, 97, 169

©Andy Ryan: pp. 20, 34, 74–75, 80, 81, 85,
99, 104, 107, 119, 133, 135, 146, 147, 165, 172,
189 (right)

©Paul Warchol: p. 33 (bottom)

This book is set in Adobe Garamond and Univers.

*This book is dedicated to our visitors, who come to these
spaces seeking something found nowhere else*

and

*To our donors, whose faith and generosity
made it all possible.*

Contents

Acknowledgments

Throughout history, architects, craftsmen, and visionaries have faced and overcome great challenges to realize monumental buildings. Their belief in ingenuity, creativity, and intellect has propelled the evolution of architecture through time. However, it is the human spirit, afforded by extraordinary individuals—benefactors, patrons, and builders—that ensures the continuing life of a building. The Bloch Building will endure, offering a portal through which we can share with future generations a glimpse of the pure expression of the human spirit.

The expansion of The Nelson-Atkins Museum of Art and the publication documenting its history are the result of the exceptional vision of many individuals, giving generously of themselves, over the past decade.

Donald J. Hall, former Chair of the Board of Trustees, member of the Building Committee, and Chair of the Architect Selection Committee, was a source of constant and unwavering support. Without his vision the project could not have been realized. Henry W. Bloch, former Chair of the Board of Trustees and past Chair of the Building Committee, provided a steadfast belief in the mission of the Museum and an abiding love for this institution. Harry McCray, Chair of the Building Committee and member of the Board of Trustees, offered steady and clear leadership of the Building Committee, whose conscientious deliberation ensured a successful conclusion to many years of oversight.

Estelle Sosland, Chair of the Board of Trustees and member of the Building Committee, partnered with the co-chairs of the Generations Capital Campaign Committee, Morton Sosland and Adele Hall, to create an unprecedented force for the Museum. Their commitment, energy, and integrity rallied the generosity of the entire Kansas City community, garnering the resources required to fund this ambitious project.

Marc F. Wilson, the Menefee D. & Mary Louise Blackwell Director/Chief Executive Officer of the Museum and Chair of the Architectural Design Oversight Committee, was the engine propelling this lofty and challenging undertaking forward with his unparalleled leadership, clear vision, and keen aesthetic sensibilities. His drive and intensity inspired those around him to strive for the best.

The Architectural Design Oversight Committee and Staff Building Committee, along with many dedicated and resilient staff members, were key to the success of the design of the Bloch Building. They devoted countless hours, conducting exhaustive analyses of every notable detail. Their combined professional expertise and enthusiasm for the collection informed each and every decision. Steve Waterman, Director, Design, and his associates Michele Boeckholt, Manager, Graphic Design, and Rebecca Young, Manager, Exhibition Design, worked tirelessly to successfully execute exhibition layout, lighting, signage, graphics, interactive technology, and the full integration of casework throughout the new building. Elisabeth Batchelor, Director, Conservation and Collections Management, was our conscience, safeguarding the Museum's collection by holding the project to high environmental and security standards. Together with her associates, Ann Erbacher, Chief Registrar, and Paul Churchill, Chief Preparator, she planned the installation of the new storage facilities and orchestrated the complex relocation of the collection. Stanley Chandler, Director, Operations, offered continuous technical expertise and oversight while keeping the existing facility operating smoothly during construction. Tim Graves and his colleagues in the Information Technology Department saw that our systems functioned seamlessly and eagerly planned for the optimum level of connectedness in the new building. Deborah Emont Scott, Chief Curator, contributed immeasurably to this effort by ensuring the primary role of the art in the evolution of the building. Also assisting were curators Jan Schall, Sanders Sosland Curator, Modern and Contemporary Art, and Keith Davis, Curator,

8

Photography, who completed ambitious installations of their respective collections. Mark Zimmerman, Director, Client Services, contributed to key components of the Bloch Building, including the new Café and the Museum Store, and readied our staff members to support our visitors. Michelle Lehrman Jenness, Manager, Security and Visitor Services, guided the design of a complex security system. She and her staff also supported seven years of construction, successfully ensuring that the visitors, the art, and the buildings always remained safe. Ann Brubaker, Director, Educational Affairs (retired), ensured the efficient and rewarding experience of all future schoolchildren, made the Spencer Art Reference Library a cornerstone of the Museum, and to much acclaim opened the new Ford Learning Center in 2004. Also contributing from Educational Affairs, Deni McHenry, Gallery Interpretation Specialist, was integral to the successful interpretation and presentation of our newly installed collections.

Karen Christiansen, Chief Operating Officer, dedicated much effort to the oversight of contract negotiation and legal issues. Her leadership, accompanied by that of Peter Hansen, former Director, External Affairs, and Barbara Head, Manager, Major Gifts, was instrumental in realizing our funding goals and preparing our organization for the future. In addition, contributing to our progress were William W. Markey, Director of Finance, and Gail Halverson Wien, Director, Human Resources. Both offered a source of support and stability while preparing for our lives after the opening.

Barbara Justus, Associate, Planning, served as construction coordinator, project writer, community liaison, staff adviser, move coordinator, tour guide, meeting organizer, and historian, among her many accomplishments throughout the course of the project. Jeff Nightingale, Assistant, Planning, took numerous photographs, documenting each stage of the construction progress. With the same vigor he conscientiously tracked the project's schedule and all expenses while providing overall support to the Planning Division. Cindy Cart, Manager, Collection Presentation and Interpretation, joined the Planning Division to skillfully orchestrate the reinstallation of the collections.

Special recognition must be given to my predecessor, Judith Cooke. Her strength of character, hard work, and notable wit were instrumental in charting the course from the beginning.

Leading the team of esteemed building professionals were Jim Lacy and Peter T. Lacy, from Lacy & Company, our Program Manager. They were ever vigilant, tracking the countless issues that accompany a project of this size. Their constancy and diplomacy drove the project forward at a steady pace.

Steven Holl provided the ingenious architectural vision, inspiring the Museum to take a leap of faith, stretching well beyond what we thought was possible. Leading this endeavor from Steven Holl Architects was Chris McVoy, assisted by Richard Tobias. Chris passionately and meticulously carried the vision to fruition. Also primary to the project's success was the work of the many dedicated design professionals at BNIM Architects, from Tom Nelson's early leadership to Casey Cassias's calm integrity that persisted in the face of any obstacle. Greg Sheldon's inexhaustible technical expertise proved unflappable even in the most challenging of design problems. Matthew Porreca's methodical observance of the design intent throughout the construction ensured the achievement of our goal.

Among the many expert designers who contributed to this project, Richard Renfro, of Renfro Design Group, Inc., and his associate Rebecca Malkin dedicated many years of detailed analysis to ensure the breathtaking use of light throughout the interior and exterior of the building. Bill Whitman and his colleagues from W. L. Cassell & Associates, Inc., strove to design to the most current museum environmental standards. Bill's honest, practical, and professional manner became a compass that guided us throughout the project. Kelley Gipple from Structural Engineering Associates exercised exhaustive care and creativity while first engineering the parking garage, then the elevator, and finally the complex web of the Bloch Building. A familiar colleague, Rick Howell, from Gould Evans Associates, ensured the continuity of our beloved Kansas City Sculpture Park, working with Steven Holl and Chris McVoy to successfully weave the landscape back together.

Faithful to the project was our general contractor, J. E. Dunn, represented by a number of determined staff led by Dan West,

9

who showed uncommon perseverance throughout the duration of the process. Dan was ably fortified by strong professionals John Hunter and, later, Eric Floyd. In the field the caliber of leadership continued with superintendents Steve Hoye and Pat Lichte. They were assisted by Richard Hoover and Charles Anderson Jr.

William P. Carter from Carter Glass Company, Inc., embodied the professional spirit of the craftspeople working on the project. Bill and his associates offered notable leadership, stepping above and beyond to ensure that the Bloch Building's glass installation met with a remarkable result.

Accompanying the completion of the Bloch Building is the publication *Stone and Feather: Steven Holl Architects / The Nelson-Atkins Museum Expansion,* a lasting tribute to the Museum's expansion endeavor and a significant contribution to the field of twenty-first-century architectural literature. First and foremost it is essential to thank Deborah Emont Scott, director of this book project. Our director, Marc F. Wilson, offered insight especially and most appreciably during the initial stages of the project, in addition to an introductory essay on the philosophy of the program that informed the design of the Bloch Building. Jeffrey Kipnis, professor of architecture at Ohio State University, provided a brilliant essay about the building and the art collection within it and its place among art museums of the twenty-first century. Steven Holl contributed the illuminating commentary on the design process and provided the source for the book's title. Chris McVoy addressed the engineering and design innovations used in the building with remarkable transparency. Roland Halbe traveled miles from Stuttgart, Germany, to take the outstanding photographs found within these pages. Using his photographic and artistic skills, he captured the building's beauty with sensitivity and clarity. Amanda Freymann, publications consultant, served as production manager and kept the project on course. Stephanie Salomon served as editor, and the book is enhanced because of her attention to detail on every page.

Bruce Campbell contributed an extraordinary design that is commensurate with that of the Bloch Building. Creatively and expertly he wove together the technical needs of the book with the artistic vision of the project. A special debt of gratitude is owed to Christopher Lyon, executive editor, Prestel Publishing, New York, who managed the book project and provided wise counsel throughout this venture.

At The Nelson-Atkins Museum, numerous staff members assisted with the details involved in the book's production. Elisabeth Batchelor, Stanley Chandler, Steve Waterman, Mark Zimmerman, and their staff members moved mountains to ready the building for photography. Karen Christiansen negotiated publication-related contracts and offered valuable advice. Jeff Nightingale stepped in and took photographs of the building when Roland Halbe could not be present. Michelle Lehrman Jenness and her staff provided assistance to Mr. Halbe as he traveled through a work in progress trying to photograph the building. Briane Lawler coordinated travel and logistics for the book project team, ensuring smooth communications and faultless scheduling.

Michele Boeckholt provided design guidance as the project moved from idea to reality. Stacey Sherman, Senior Coordinator, Rights and Reproductions, assured that Jeffrey Kipnis's essay was properly illustrated by securing the appropriate photographs. Lara Kline, Manager, and Toni Wood, Assistant Manager, Marketing and Communications, provided editorial counsel.

For generously funding this publication we thank The Nelson Gallery Foundation.

Finally, along with the individuals included here, many others offered significant contributions to the success of the Bloch Building, the publication, and the future of The Nelson-Atkins Museum of Art. We are grateful to them all.

Dana M. Knapp
Director, Planning, and Project Director

Stone & *Feather*

Rethinking One Art Museum

Marc F. Wilson

Menefee D. & Mary Louise Blackwell Director/CEO

For the past twenty or so years the world has struggled to establish new institutional paradigms for a new global civilization. Art museums have been caught in the crosscurrents. Nowhere has the struggle been more evident than in the United States, where art museum expansions pepper the landscape. The vigor and ambition signaled by this explosion of construction are welcome and promise a positive future for cultural activities. The results, however, bespeak an atomization of values, a fragmentation of consensus about the role of art museums in society, and uncertainty about the relationship between the art museum and its visitors.

It is no doubt difficult to make sense of a tornado of change when you are in the eye of it. But what is astonishing is the willingness, even eagerness, of normally conservative sponsors of these new structures to adopt risky architectural gambits while in the midst of what can be thought of as a perfect storm of civic ego, commerce, and a general public increasingly inclined to superficial gratification. Viewed from the perspectives of architectural invention and sound museum practice, absurdity of architectural form frequently seems to have triumphed over thoughtful restraint, while practical considerations seem hardly to have been entertained in many instances. What we see too often is an unhappy bundle of unbridled extravagance and unmindful neglect of essentials.

Those who would undertake to build a new art museum, as we and Steven Holl Architects did in 1999, must first recognize the new world we are dealing with, one marked by social and cultural shifts with roots that are deep and complex. Building a new art museum means addressing these major social and behavioral issues if the effort is to be successful, defined as offering gratifying personal experiences that prompt return visits. These issues too often have gone underappreciated as museum leaders focused more on achieving celebrity status for the new building

and on generating earned income for the institution and home city by stimulating tourist spending. The seductiveness of these goals to civic egos and commercial interests has been well recognized in current critical literature for what they are: short-term returns, usually overestimated and not sustainable. The core business of an art museum must continue to be putting people in touch with inspiring works of art that matter to us when we look at them.

It has become commonplace to take to task the narcissistic formal extravagances that mark a number of recently completed projects. What is not so well recognized is the overwhelming attention that has been paid to the exteriors, which is a clear consequence of straining for celebrity status by architectural means. Galleries and exhibition spaces have been given short shrift, left nondescript and sometimes poorly finished, hardly environments conducive to the deeply rewarding, transformative dialogue with works of art that art museums are expected to deliver.

At the heart of the matter lies an ongoing redefinition of the relationship between the visitor (all visitors, each visitor) and the experience of works of art. If the chances of long-term success for a new art museum building are to be improved, responsible parties must broaden their considerations and revise the balance of priorities. The essential business of the art museum must be the central concern when it comes time to reexamine core values, set strategies and goals, and, finally, select an architect. The architect must not be called upon to figure out who you want to be. That critical task, which is much more than space planning, belongs to the museum.

Escaping the Taxonomic Straitjacket

On the whole, art museums have failed to adapt the presentation of works of art to the changed audiences and changed expectations that have accompanied the long-term growth of attendance

[facing page] Aerial view to the southwest of the Bloch and Nelson-Atkins buildings. At the lower right is the J.C. Nichols Plaza and Walter De Maria's *One Sun / 34 Moons.*

14

(surely a welcome development). While audiences have changed dramatically, the conceptual foundations upon which art museums develop and construct the presentation of their collections have gradually, perhaps imperceptibly, fossilized into a taxonomic straitjacket that has evolved with increasing elaboration and rigidity over the past 250 years.

The taxonomy of art history shares its origins with systems of classification developed for the natural sciences. Scholarship in art history has pursued splitting of categories into ever smaller, ever more narrowly defined inquiry, which has tended to fracture understanding of "big pictures" into dendritic models that move toward ever finer distinctions. Inquiry moves further from the trunks and major branches of synthetic understanding to the twigs of minutiae. It is not that this model of inquiry is not fruitful. It is, but it is more a matter of balance and the need for

synthetic construction of newly conceived "wholes." The ultimate goal of "splitting" is to create a new "whole."

Traditionally art museums rely on the taxonomy of art history as the general template for the conceptual organization of exhibitions. But art history and collateral disciplines are tools to be employed in crafting presentations meaningful to a broadly, inclusively defined audience. When the tool is mistaken for the goal, the public will either be left behind or put off by the irrelevance of academic hairsplitting to its own expectations, wants, and background. This phenomenon is seen often enough in large, comprehensive exhibitions, where a march from case to case, from object to object, becomes an endurance trial in which meaning does not reside in an experience with the objects individually and then collectively, but rather in grasping and in finding meaning in fine distinctions.

There appears to be an unspoken goal that a successful experience with the display will turn the visitor into the curator. The display and the visitor are conceived as being on the same wavelength; never mind that this is of concern to a small fraction of the audience and is irrelevant to the needs of the majority of the audience. This approach may work for the specialist, the collector, and the aficionado, but it fails the rest of us. The biggest loser is the work of art, whose preeminent role is to generate a richly rewarding aesthetic experience for the visitor, who, with modest expenditures of effort and native intelligence, can enter into a personal dialogue with the art.

The Changing Public

As we rethink the art museum, we must understand and deal with changes in the makeup and expectations of audiences. It is clear in our society that art museums, as is the case with non-profit organizations in general, exist to facilitate beneficial change in the lives of people. We do, however, face audiences that on the whole are less well prepared to deal with historical material.

Not so long ago, public education provided basic preparation for experiencing the visual arts, skill in the expressive conventions of language, and a respectful acquaintance with events of the past and the processes of history, all of which were held to be essential for the citizen at large to navigate the present successfully and to contribute to a better future for a democratic society. The gradual simplification of public language and of the presentation of complex issues in our public media over the past three decades testifies to the low expectations we now have of our citizens, which unfortunately has affected similarly our estimation of the museum audience.

Dramatic changes in values have validated a society whose members may live in the moment and for the moment with little sense of the importance of the past in shaping the present or of the connectedness of our current circumstances to the past. Until recently the generally accepted view of art museums in America held that they were "civilizing"; that is, their collections and activities contributed to advancing learning and social norms. This evaluation rested on the belief that the past was instructive

and that it could even serve up wisdom if we attuned ourselves to its messages. When the past and what can be learned from its study are no longer esteemed or even thought of as possibly relevant to today's circumstances, institutions meant to treasure past achievement for the sake of benefit to the present and future will have a tough time making a case for the importance of the experience to be had between an individual visitor and the human genius embodied in works of art.

Among the consequences of postmodernism and deconstructivism has been the devaluing of history as a resource for understanding the present. History has always been manipulated to serve current goals (usually political), but many of us are wary and weary of the abject dishonesty and unabashed hypocrisy used to justify the recent manipulations of the past. Norms and normative institutions, once deconstructed, are not easily replaced. And in their place are mostly contention and confusion.

It Takes Two to Tango

One other factor bearing on the visitor's experience needs to be discussed. This has to do not with what the visitor expects of the museum experience but what he expects of himself. Should the visitor be held in some measure responsible for contributing to the success of a visit to the art museum? May we expect the visitor to meet us half way? Part way? Some of the way? I subscribe to the belief that there is more to life than being a spectator. From the audience I expect a willingness to be open to new experiences and to make an effort to engage in the possibilities that might be found in an experiential encounter with works of art.

Within a generation, we have seen a ferocious assertion of individuality in social behavior and in attitudes toward authority of any kind. This has carried over into expectations of public institutions, including those like the art museum that deal essentially in personal experiences. Anything suggestive of authority, be it interpretation or even recommended paths to further personal gratification, is first viewed suspiciously, then often dismissed with fashionable glibness as being canonical or elitist, meaning that the item in question challenges one's sense of self, sense of identity, and rightful place in the world, which in the end may depend on nothing more than the fact of one's existence and on the morality in which we have bundled ourselves for the sake of emotional security. The fragile ego, cocooned in touchy individualism, makes for difficult communication.

Today's visitors, then, arrive at the art museum with a broad spectrum of expectations, core values, and education, and we must be prepared to offer each a rewarding experience with great works of art. An art museum's leaders must know what the institution means to its own community, the region, and the world. They must understand the complexities of the visitors and the modern interaction with art. The works of art, ultimately, with their stories to tell and the passions they ignite, must be made more intellectually and emotionally accessible to people who walk through the doors of the museum. At the Nelson-Atkins, we began by knowing who we were, then moved forward with what we wanted to become.

Shaping the Future

As we open the new Bloch Building of the Nelson-Atkins, our first addition ever, we must emphasize that the physical expansion represented by the new building, along with the reconfiguration and repurposing of spaces within the existing Nelson-Atkins Building and the physical renovation of the Kansas City Sculpture Park, are strategic moves within a much grander set of strategies and goals developed during the 1990s, completed in 1997, and adopted by the Museum's Board of Trustees in April 1998. Seen in this context, the addition of a large wing to an existing building is a tool, not a goal in and of itself. The expansion thus expresses very specific program goals and operational requirements. These must be met fully if the new wing is to be declared a success, no matter how photogenic the building might be.

The Nelson-Atkins strategic plan is not so much a road map as a set of concise statements of carefully interwoven goals intended to make the Museum more useful to its varied publics, both traditional and evolving. The goals demand sweeping reassessment of everything the Museum does. Fundamentals of values and of purpose, seen in an especially dynamic context

within a greater American mandate, were challenged, examined, and recast. The centrality of the visitor's experiences with works of art was reaffirmed as the main business, the principal "product," of the institution. It also confirmed that this Museum's art collection is the enduring asset of the museum, which, if managed well, will only get better and become more effective with the passing of time.

Determining the Program

The goals of the plan determined the architectural program. That is, the strategic plan's goals determined what the expansion, the reconfiguration, and the renovations would be expected to accomplish. Once the goals were agreed upon, quantification of space requirements was begun under the professional guidance of E. Verner Johnson and Associates. Determination of quantitative requirements went hand in hand with qualitative analysis of particular spaces, and of spatial relationships and adjacencies, all with an eye toward facilitating visitors' experiences and ease of operations.

Two factors are especially salient in accounting for the architectural requirements. One of these is the inclusive nature of the strategic planning process itself. It was not a top-down effort, but rather solicited input from a truly broad range of sectors that make up the greater Kansas City community. Taxi drivers, elected officials, all levels of educators and administrators within Kansas City's multi-state sprawling educational establishment, artists and collectors, leaders in business and commerce, Museum donors and members, and staff and trustees were all canvassed for input. So, too, were opinions and views sought from leaders in the art worlds of surrounding cities. The Museum serves a sparsely populated but vast territory stretching westward from the middle of Missouri on the east to the Colorado border on the west, and from Des Moines, Omaha, and Lincoln on the north to Oklahoma City, Tulsa, Joplin, and Springfield on the south. Put simply, the Nelson-Atkins carries a responsibility to serve major Midwestern cities in a geographical area of roughly 600 by 300 miles. The mandate for the Museum to be encyclopedic thus becomes clear.

Gathering input was followed by architectural programming, which in a very abstract way sorts out quantities, qualitative issues, relationships, and priorities. This is the phase when political horse-trading among different agendas and perspectives gets settled. Only after this stage did we begin the process of selecting an architect. We knew who we were and wanted to be; and we had defined diagrammatically what that meant in terms of expansion, reconfiguration, and renovation.

Seen in this light, the Bloch Building is one strategy among many in a four-phase project that touches every corner of the grounds and every practice and procedure. No one and no thing has been left out. For example, the stunning expansion of space for education activities is a direct outcome of our communities' desire for more educational programming, in the expectation that the Nelson-Atkins's distinguished collections could become more meaningful to visitors of all backgrounds. Thus the Ford Learning Center, which includes several classrooms and an Educator Resource Center, now occupies three-fourths of the ground floor of the original Nelson-Atkins Building. The Spencer Art Reference Library, the largest of its kind between Chicago and Berkeley, has a new home at the top level of the lobby lens in the Bloch Building, where it is easily accessed. Reference librarians have been added and public hours doubled.

Hidden from View
Often overlooked by visitors and by reviews and media stories about a new art museum building are the resources and space devoted to support services. Beneath the public spaces of the Bloch Building is an equally large and even more complex cluster of facilities known to insiders as "The City," which houses loading docks, storerooms, and crating areas, among other areas. Mechanical rooms must be provided, especially if they are not to intrude on areas devoted to galleries, interrupting ideal patterns of circulation. The Museum is like an iceberg. Only the top is exposed, with the vast portion that keeps the whole thing afloat hidden from view.

Much effort and money went into designing, building, and equipping support facilities. Long-term issues of efficiency and

of manpower requirements were examined and designs were chosen that minimized the need for additional resources, especially human resources, which make up the largest part of the budget. There is no free lunch, and the imperative of long-term economy may entail capital-intensive investment upfront.

To state that the Bloch Building contains 165,000 square feet of interior space fails to capture the actual dimensions of its construction. Add to that total another 55,000 square feet of outdoor "park-gallery" space constructed on the roofs of the interior gallery spaces. Nothing in viewers' past experience prepares them for this spatial relationship, that above the gallery where I am enjoying a painting by Willem de Kooning or a Benin head, other visitors are outside experiencing the lenses as sculptures in their own right, in a landscape that also accommodates in happy sympathy works by George Segal, Ursula von Rydingsvard, and Tony Cragg. Pets and naps are welcome here.

Enabling the Visitor's Experience
Several principles involving the new addition and the visitor's experience outside the buildings were mandated in the architectural program given to finalists in the design competition. One of these principles focused on clarity of information and options conveyed to visitors, beginning not after the visitor has entered the building, but miles away, with good directional signage along major traffic arteries. Next in our hypothetical visitor's mind must be certainty that he or she has arrived at the right place, the intended destination. It must be clear how to enter and where to park. Clarity of way finding is a governing principle. Keeping the visitor upbeat, in a good mood and free of frustration, are the umbrella goals that informed so many of our design directives.

Further design mandates were intended to preserve what was beloved by the public in the existing building and in the surrounding Kansas City Sculpture Park. The Kansas City community made it clear that the iconic neoclassical building from 1933 must not be marginalized in any way by an expansion. Nor could we destroy the park by displacing trees, shrubs, and grass with lifeless construction. The community's notion of marginalization went beyond physical and aesthetic encroachment to embrace elements of memory and emotional import. Kirkwood Hall, one of the grandest reception halls in an American museum, had to remain the spiritual and ceremonial heart of the new museum complex.

Finding the Solution

Steven Holl and his team arrived at a brilliant solution that completely fulfilled the requirements of the Museum's strategic plan and its architectural program while responding creatively to the injunctions of the community. To the east facade of the centralized, orthogonally composed original neoclassical building he attached a slender structure, 840 feet long, which runs downhill. The existing east facade of the building, above the ground floor, was preserved by connecting the new structure to the east side entrance of the existing building at ground level, thus leaving major north, south, and west facades as they were, while the grand portico of the east face is framed by a gap in the lens structures of the new building. Much of the new construction was placed underground or, if above the original grade, was made to seem an integral element of the park by wrapping grass, shrubs, and paths over and around the structure, thus preserving the park and not impairing its use

The trickiest problem grew out of the mandate to make the new and old structures function as one in terms of circulation and logical flow of spaces, an issue whose difficulty was exacerbated by moving lobby functions from the central hall (Kirkwood Hall) of the existing neoclassical building to a new multistoried lobby building. How to provide effortless circulation, clarity of way finding, and aesthetic compatibility between old and new was met by the ingenious observation of Chris McVoy, project architect and partner-in-charge, that a grand, architecturally sumptuous passageway between the new Bloch lobby and Kirkwood Hall could be constructed by extending a grand stairway through existing walls to link with a large space that formerly had served as a special exhibition gallery. The result is a spectacular view that sweeps upward from the Bloch Building lobby beyond a grand marble staircase into a classicizing forecourt, which opens onto Kirkwood Hall. For the long-time Kansas City resident, being able to glimpse Kirkwood's majestic black marble columns was reassuring. For those of us designing the construction, the results demonstrated our sensitivity to the iconic existing building.

Issues of parking, entry, security, and weather prompted the decision to turn the parking garage into one of the entry experiences, and not simply a space for the short-term warehousing of cars. The usual vehicular dungeon, with a crummy connection to the main architectural event, would not do. Instead, visitors arriving by car (which most do) park beneath the J.C. Nichols Plaza and reflecting pool. Shimmering natural light cast into the garage through the "moons" of Walter De Maria's *One Sun / 34 Moons* intrigues visitors as they make their way to the building.

Throughout the design phase Steven Holl and Chris McVoy adopted a strategy of deferring to the original building. Whether in shape, material, or scale, this deference not only governs but also goes beyond normal expectations by compelling visitors to have a relationship with the existing building unlike what was possible in the past. This new relationship is much more vigorous because it is strengthened by strategies that alternate between focus and contrast. The poignancy of the juxtapositions of old and new emerges in recognition of how and where the buildings are similar. The grand temple of 1933 has emerged refreshed thanks to its sympathetic new partner.

Design for the Visitor

The visitor's expectations and needs were continually at the forefront of our consciousness as we designed and planned. What could architecture, space, and time do to facilitate a gratifying personal experience with works of art?

I do not believe in the so-called neutral environment. Environments are never neutral; they always affect us. The modern embrace of the white box as an ideal environment— no personality, just neutrality— is really something of a hoax. First, white is not neutral. It is among the most aggressive of colors, draining color out of anything hung against it, as anyone who has hung a Monet landscape on a flat white wall knows. Architects like white because it tends to turn light into planes, to

Visitors, art, and architecture come together in a contemporary gallery of the Bloch Building.

architectural design intended to support a dialogue between the visitor and the works of art. The gallery spaces in the Bloch Building have not been designed with homogeneous, all-purpose flexibility in mind. They have been designed specifically to accommodate sympathetically the types of works to be shown in them.

For example, the spaces for the photography galleries are intimate in scale. Formal activity is subdued and elegant. Wall color and values change from dark to light as the display of works progresses chronologically. The organization of the installation and of the spaces mirror one another. They were conceived that way from the start. Within the world of photography, the gallery architecture is flexible enough to accommodate all known needs.

The African art gallery is even more specific in marrying the presentation of art with the enclosing architecture. Here all is seamlessly one, with little perceptible sense that the room is an independent envelope into which exhibition casework has been fitted. Exhibition furniture is architecture, and architecture is exhibition furniture.

While the goal is to provide an environment that supports the connection between the visitor and the work of art, the "theater" of casework, lighting, and architecture must disappear as the visitor focuses attention on a work of art. To the extent possible, all barriers to a full experience must be and have been eliminated. For example, the Nelson-Atkins has invested heavily in new glass technology that virtually eliminates awareness of casework glass as a physical and psychological barrier between the visitor and the work of art. Taking a cue from Steven Holl's palette of materials, glass has been employed structurally in the fabrication of casework in order to integrate seamlessly Holl's architecture and the Museum's installations.

While being supportive, architecture and casework may not be distracting or in any way overwhelm the works of art displayed within. These same governing principles apply to the Museum's interpretive materials, which must never compete with the work of art but must lead the visitor back to it with new keys for understanding.

In designing with the "golden triangle" in mind, it is clear that the behavioral responses that the visitor is likely to have

emphasize monolithic planarity, which in turn has a forceful influence over how planes and spaces are perceived. Boxes can be good or bad, depending on proportions and scale.

The architectural environment of the art museum should be designed to support the visitor's experiences with the works of art. Nowhere is this more critical than in the design of gallery spaces and in the presentation of works of art within them. The visitor, the architectural environment, and the works of art make up a triangular model of interests that must be accommodated synergistically, a museological version of mathematics' "golden triangle." The Nelson-Atkins has adopted strategies for that triangle that multiply opportunities for each angle to amplify the others.

Once major exterior issues of design were resolved at a macro level, gallery spaces were designed from the inside out, with the

must be incorporated into design considerations. The experience of a work of art is first of all a sensory, visual experience. It is aesthetic in nature and in the course of the experience, cognitive and emotive reactions blend and memory comes into play as well. In reality, cognitive faculties and emotive faculties are never discrete departments but constantly interact, like *yin* and *yang*. Other essential factors include recognition that the aesthetic experience is personal and that it will vary with the intelligence, visual sophistication, background, and interests of the individual. This is not to say that we are dealing with a free-for-all of subjectivity. Human behavior and personal response are still subject to categorization and prediction.

As we think about how to multiply opportunities for connections between visitors and works of art, it helps to focus on the essentials of the aesthetic experience. Too often museums smother the visitors' faculties by displaying too many objects that are only marginally able to generate a gratifying aesthetic experience. The impulse to present a complete taxonomic picture is apparently difficult to resist.

The "Presence" of Art

At the Nelson-Atkins Museum, we believe in editing our displays in a demanding way, according to the "less-is-more" principle. Only those works that have what we call "presence"—the power to communicate forcefully with broad audiences through visual terms—are chosen. Remembering that art history is a tool, not a goal, we try not to give in to the temptation to illustrate the history of art as concocted in the latest textbook on the subject. High points of visual achievement stand a much better chance of communicating with more people, in more meaningful ways, than second-rate works. Selection is not about name, fame, or dollar value. It is all about presence—all about the extraordinary achievement in visual expression of one human genius connecting with the receptive genius of another.

Multiplying opportunities for personal engagement was a key strategy for the Nelson-Atkins. Every aesthetic experience should enlarge the experiential capacities of the viewer; every display should lead to attractive options for further gratifying and enlarging experience. Creating a spatial dynamic that holds out indefinite possibilities or "becomings" is a characteristic we and Steven Holl Architects sought. No two rooms are the same. The static box is avoided in favor of asymmetry and an equilibrium of resolved imbalance. As walls kink, or intersect at odd angles, ceilings fold and bend, and light levels brighten or dim, a gentle dynamic awakens the visitor to indefinite interpretation of what may be or could happen in the spaces ahead. Light is meant to be dynamic, not static or homogeneous. This is the difference between a Gregorian chant and a lyric opera.

The 1933 Nelson-Atkins Building is a perfect example of symmetry and balance. Something symmetrical is static, its visual forces perfectly resolved. Rhythmic forces cancel one another. What we have tried to achieve in the Bloch Building is the refreshing, enlivening energy that comes of spaces that flow, that have unresolved rhythmic force and movement springing from asymmetry and imbalance. Neither we nor Steven Holl Architects believe in the homogeneous space and time of the Renaissance. Space and time are both elastic. Steven Holl and Chris McVoy make elasticity palpable. The dynamics of light and space actually speed or slow the visitor's pace. These features play into our thinking about the organization of our presenta-

tions of works of art. The dynamics of open-ended possibilities have found their way into how we think about structuring relationships (and therefore meaning) among works we wish to display. The works themselves set the messages to be conveyed. Thus, asymmetrical clustering orders the presentation of the collections in harmonic resonance with Steven Holl's dynamic, elastic spaces. While this dynamic is intended to multiply windows of access, cognitively and emotively, it must be guided so as not to risk busyness. The overall emotional force of the environment and of the exhibitions is one of calm.

The full effect of the Bloch Building will reveal itself over time. But it has already provided a rich and powerful experience for those of us who thought about the Nelson-Atkins in a global sense, who considered the Museum's role in modern society and who ventured to transform an art museum in the middle of the nation's heartland. If we have been successful, visitors will return often. We are betting that the architectural environment and the presentation of the works of art create a meaningful experience, that visitors will connect with the genius of others through works of art, and that the aesthetic experience will be enjoyable and enlarging in ways that are cumulative over the life of a person. The rest is history.

...and Then, Something Magical

Jeffrey Kipnis

July 8, 1999, *Kansas City Star*: "The Nelson-Atkins Museum of Art has picked American architect Steven Holl, widely considered a rising star in the profession, to design an $80 million addition to the original 1933 Building. ….'At the end of the day, this stood out as something that was magical,' Nelson-Atkins director Marc Wilson said of the Holl scheme."

Even if you have never been to Kansas City and your only experience of Steven Holl and Chris McVoy's[1] design for an addition to The Nelson-Atkins Museum comes from the photographs you are browsing, you can still sense how prophetic Marc Wilson's remark was. There *is* something magical about the architecture. Most obviously, the Bloch Building enchants the night as its stark floes of frozen light, afloat on swells of landscape, draft the darkness into a chiaroscuro so vast that it cannot exist, still so real that you can touch it. Yet, that act of wizardry is but one of many the architecture performs, and if the most stunning, not nearly the most fascinating.

For example, for those familiar with the Nelson-Atkins collection, the building's operatic night countenance may bring to mind a similar drama of darkness and light staged in Caravaggio's painting *Saint John the Baptist in the Wilderness*. If so, then another of the powers of the building will have already begun to unfold; we can get a hint of it with a little trick of our own. First, let us read a portion of the description that accompanies the painting, one of the museum's most prized masterpieces:

[Caravaggio] has literally stripped the Baptist of nearly all traditional attributes (halo, lamb and banderole inscribed *Ecce Agnus Dei* or Behold the Lamb of God), leaving the brooding intensity of his emotional state as the subject of the painting. Saint John's solemn pensiveness is reinforced by a Caravaggio trademark: the dramatic contrast of deep, opaque shadows, playing across the body and shrouding the sockets of the eyes, with a bright light that illuminates the Baptist from above and to his right. This stark contrast

of light and darkness, the brilliant scarlet of the saint's cloak and Caravaggio's placement of him in the foreground close to our own space, all contribute to the dramatic impact of the painting.

Now, on a whim, let us revise the passage ever so slightly:

Holl has literally stripped the building of nearly all the traditional attributes of a museum, leaving only the emotional intensity of its mute light-forms. The ensemble's taut silence is reinforced by a trademark of Caravaggio: the dramatic contrast of deep, opaque shadows with bright light. This stark contrast of light and darkness staged on a draped cloak of landscape, the scattered placement of the addition's abstract forms so close to the original building, all contribute to the dramatic impact of the architecture.

[right] Michelangelo Merisi, called Caravaggio, Italian (1571–1610). *Saint John the Baptist in the Wilderness*, 1604–05. Oil on canvas, 68 x 52 in. (172.72 x 132.08 cm). The Nelson-Atkins Museum of Art, Kansas City, Missouri. Purchase: Nelson Trust, 52-25.

[facing page] View to the northeast of Nelson-Atkins and Bloch buildings at night.

Broadly speaking and independent of aesthetic issues, architectural history has developed three distinct approaches to consider the ways in which architecture can say something about the world: intellectual, social, and phenomenological. An intellectual approach conceives of the building as an object of formal contemplation that communicates through conscious understanding and interpretation. For example, one might understand a shift or rotation in the building as completing patterns or making alignments with other features in the context. The social approach focuses on how a building communicates through its institutional role. Should an art museum resemble a temple, a palace, or a warehouse? There is no correct answer. Rather, each is an option that speaks differently about the nature of art and our relation to it, and all are at work in the Nelson-Atkins expansion.

The phenomenological approach sees the building as a knot of blended perceptions that communicate simultaneously through sensation, intuition, and comprehension to produce a place in the world. To an architect so inclined, the echo of footfall on paving stone is important, not as pure experience, but as a contribution to place in all of its specificities. In a cathedral it engenders meditative solitude, in a court of law, respectful obedience, on a dark and abandoned city street, fear. While every building contains aspects of all three of these approaches, architects disposed to explore new possibilities tend to bias their speculations toward one or another. In the case of Steven Holl, the architect is strongly inclined toward the phenomenological.

The term *phenomenology* is used somewhat differently in architecture than it is in philosophy, where the architectural connotation would be more akin to existential phenomenology. The architectural sense of the term derives primarily from the writings of philosophers Martin Heidegger and Maurice Merleau-Ponty. Because Holl draws heavily on the latter rather than the former, a brief excursion into the differences between the two might shed some light on the architect's work in the Nelson-Atkins expansion.

In elementary terms, Heidegger distinguishes the authentic being of our world from its everyday appearances, which he sees as fraught with inauthenticity. For example, he finds in the lure of technology an escape into inauthenticity, and seeks to return our lives to a more genuine relationship with the world of being. Merleau-Ponty rejects his colleague's position that meaning and authenticity arise from a metaphysical relationship between appearances and being, preferring to inquire how these evolve from the perceptions of a body living in a world as phenomena. To ground his discourse thoroughly in perceptions, he discusses the interplay of things, experiences, and ideas in terms of the *visible* and *invisible*, emphasizing the way these two interact with and change each other, calling attention to what he calls the "profound carnality of their doubling." In this view, meaning and the material world are inherent in each other.

Above all Merleau-Ponty affirms the primacy of a pre-intellectual kinship between us and the world of perception that is more fundamental than our thinking capacities. He holds that at any point in time, the human situation is a product of both the mind and socio-historical circumstance, implying, in contrast to Heidegger, that everyday life might collaborate with the forces of change to produce new authenticities of a different order, existential authenticities as deep-seated and timeless as "being" in its own way, yet inseparable from history and place. Because intellectual thought in and of itself can never apprehend such an authenticity, the ineluctable role of the arts in any quest to catch awareness of this elusive prize becomes evident.

Yet, who is to say which aspects of life at any moment are authentic and which are not? How can one possibly tell at what point technology, commerce, media, and all of the other dizzying sources of change in our lives have given rise to a new and genuine authenticity, when they seem inexorably to lead us away from authenticity as such? Surely in the century since its invention, incandescent lighting has become for us a new kind of natural light, its 60-cycle-per-second song—B-flat two octaves below middle C—as much a part of our nature as its signature yellow. But are the social networks now proliferating on the Internet also authentic, when face-to-face social encounters were once the sine qua non of an authentic community? It is precisely the fascinating uncertainties contained in such questions that motivate the speculative design decisions of architects like Holl.

From a historical perspective, of course, a comparison of two such disparate works is mere caprice. Yet if we linger on the painting and an aerial view of the addition, we see that the conversation between the two continues well beyond the play of light and dark, reaching to the respective forms, organization, and the sense of space. If we let our imagination run free, we can picture the original building as the Baptist's head, the new addition as his left arm, and the great lawn as his chest. The staid neoclassical facade seems to mirror the pensive symmetry of darkened eyes above a highlighted, aquiline nose. The shoulder hunching toward the head suggests the tense crowding of the original by the addition, while the sequence of over-lit muscles in the arm becomes the new building's "lenses," the form of the last lens reiterating the bend of the arm at the elbow. Even the terraces of the great lawn reverberate in the Baptist's rib-rippled chest.

As we further explore the architecture, other conversations between the building and works of art will attract our attention. Indeed, an integral part of the architecture itself is a new artwork that graces the reflecting pool, *One Sun / 34 Moons*, by Walter De Maria in collaboration with Steven Holl. As fun as it will be to eavesdrop on these, however, they cannot be the most important of its relationships—after all, the Bloch wing joins not only an institution with a staff and a beautiful existing building, but a local community and a city. It joins as well the history and current practice of architecture and in the end participates in the world at large. It enters into dialogues in each and every one of these arenas; but, since the same is true for every building, the multiplicity of its conversations is not what makes its architectural achievement so extraordinary. Rather, its special magic derives from what it has to say, and even more, from how it goes about saying it.

We have already noticed that the Bloch Building possesses none of the symbolic trappings that architects customarily use to identify an important civic or cultural edifice, such as those so in evidence in the majestic neoclassical facade of the 1933 Nelson-Atkins Building. With the exception of the two revolving doors at the front entry off the fountain plaza that from a distance appear to be oversized column stubs—a nod to the great columnar entrance of its elder colleague—the new wing not only lacks a ceremonial facade, but even an exterior marquee bearing its name.

As Caravaggio humanizes John and thus makes his spiritual struggle more palpable, Holl relaxes the formality of the museum to sponsor a more personal rapport between viewer and art. The older building does everything in its power to engender a distanced formality between viewer and art, in keeping with the custom of its time. In her book *The Nelson-Atkins Museum of Art*,[2] Kristie Wolferman makes it clear that the benefactors, trustees, and architects who midwifed the museum all wanted the building be "part temple, part monument."

Although the grand bearing and hallowed tone projected by the neoclassical architecture of the 1933 building might seem to some overly affected today, these traits were not merely custom, but de rigueur for civic museums in the United States at the time. Wolferman traces this stylistic imperative to the triumph of New York's Metropolitan Museum of Art and lists some twenty-two American museums—from Boston to Cleveland to Omaha— built under its sway. Even though architecture's modern movement was by then already in full blossom as the International Style, the United States would not see a modern museum building until 1939, when Edward Durell Stone's Museum of Modern Art opened in New York.

To design the original Nelson-Atkins, Thomas Wight, principal of the Kansas City firm Wight and Wight, turned to the Cleveland Museum of 1916 as a model. The resemblance between the two buildings and their settings is quite striking, except that the Cleveland is built of white marble, while the Nelson-Atkins is in limestone, making a comparison an object lesson on the effects of materiality. In 1970, the Cleveland Museum expanded with a program similar to that of the Bloch Building and chose Marcel Breuer, best known for his Whitney Museum of American Art in New York, to design the addition. Breuer, a staunch advocate of modern architecture's rejection of historical styles, was the preeminent practitioner in the United States of a subgenre of modern architecture named Brutalism, after its predilection for austere geometry built in raw concrete or rough-hewn stone. In a tour de force of architectural one-upmanship,

Breuer effectively relegated the 1916 building to the status of picture postcard kitsch by erecting a modern monument so powerful that it confiscated the dignity of the original.

Two artists similarly discomfited by the pretensions of the original Nelson-Atkins Museum and grounds are the team Claes Oldenburg and Coosje van Bruggen, whose large-scale sculpture *Shuttlecocks* lampoons not so much the building's style as its social implications, in the great tradition of political satire. In so doing, the artists revisit a long-standing debate in the arts over whether or not a symbolic form is indelibly wed to its original content. Unwilling to dissociate the neoclassical architecture from its affiliation with the class-based society in which it originated, the artists level a mischievous critique at it. In part its jab at wealth and power is made broadly in the name of democracy (though with some tongue in cheek, given badminton's own class associations). But more to the point, it is a jab at the mien of authority the building conveys, made in defense of the right of each of us to expect our opinion to be valued when it comes to art.

However one feels about the *Shuttlecocks*, one cannot deny the economy of its critical genius. When its burlesque on scale and manners casts the art, the garden grounds, and building as a badminton court, it unites all three of the major public components of the institution as a single target in its crosshairs. If nothing else, it reminds us that very few art institutions have so interwoven their architecture, grounds, and art into one social experience as the Nelson-Atkins, a fact that will grow in significance as we turn back to the Bloch Building.

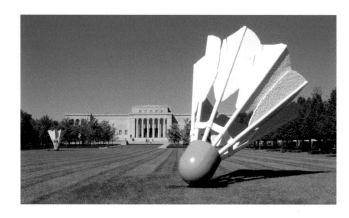

The Kansas City Sculpture Park at The Nelson-Atkins Museum of Art with two of four *Shuttlecocks* by Claes Oldenburg, American (b. Sweden, 1929) and Coosje van Bruggen, American (b. The Netherlands, 1942), 1994. Aluminum, fiberglass-reinforced plastic, paint, 230 9/16 x 191 7/8 in. (585.63 x 487.36 cm). Purchase: acquired through the generosity of the Sosland Family, F94-1/3,4.

If in his approach to the original building Holl identifies with Breuer's modernist bent and joins Oldenburg and van Bruggen's egalitarian advocacy, his design for the new addition does so not in the spirit of competition or critique, but with tender cunning, one of the work's hallmark achievements. The architecture uses submissiveness, flattery, and gifts to seduce the original institution into a new political posture and a more contemporary attitude in its presentation of the collection. With a few sleights of hand so brilliant-quick that they are all but impossible to catch, he turns the Wight building both into a partner and into a new work of art, an unexpected "recent acquisition" for the collection.

Just consider the episode that occurs when one climbs the staircase from the gardens to the narrow gap between the first lens and the east facade of the old building. Coming from the gardens, already receptive to viewing things as sculpture, we climb toward an Ionic column of the original building framed as sculpture, with the staircase landing as its pedestal. It is reminiscence in miniature of the notorious staging of the *Nike of Samothrace* on the Daru staircase in the Louvre.[3] The proximity of the old and new buildings at this point compresses the viewer close to the column, insisting on attention to the bracelet of Egyptian lotus ornament etched at the bottom of the shaft of the columns. The column has never been so lovely, particularly if one remembers that before the addition, the base of these columns stood twelve feet off the ground, landing above the entry doors to the east wing.

This difference in approach is part and parcel of the distinction between a conceptual and a phenomenological work. For the *Shuttlecocks* to perform at a political level, its message must be read and understood. Holl's architecture on the other hand, works its wiles more patiently, weaving an intricate tapestry of perceptions and intuitions with meditation and flashes of insight. Every ounce of the expansion—from the parking lot to the galleries, to the grass mounds and walkways—plays an important part, as does every mood, thought, and manner of attention it solicits from a visitor. On the one hand, it assists the traditional modes of close attention associated with the institution: the alert scrutiny of the critic, the passionate concentration

of the connoisseur, or the remove of the historian. But it also supports modes of attention to the art loosened from objectivity to wander aimlessly in reverie and daydream. Misunderstanding, confusion, even utter distraction have their place here alongside understanding and concentration. As a result in the expanded museum politics recedes as a distinct polemic to become instead part of a new way of being in the world, one in which the freedom from unwarranted authority is felt as much as understood.

The Gifts

About a year before joining the original building at its side, the Bloch Building sent tributes, a beautiful plaza and reflecting pool, Walter De Maria's *One Sun / 34 Moons,* and a new underground parking facility. In addition to their undeniable value, these shrewd gifts helped set the stage for an amiable relationship between the two.

When in 1829 Johann Wolfgang von Goethe called architecture frozen music, he inscribed one of the most enduring plati-

tudes about any art form into our cultural consciousness. If threadbare, it still rings with truth, particularly when one thinks of classical styles in both arts—the rousing overture of facades, the rhythms of regal symmetries, the intricate counterpoint of plans, and symphonic climaxes of spaces as superbly portrayed in Thomas Wight's rendition of the original Nelson-Atkins Museum. The plaza and reflecting pool fit easily into the neoclassical style of Wight's edifice, and begin the process of creating for it a stately forecourt that the first lens of the Bloch would complete upon arrival. As long as the first lens faces the plaza, it maintains the orthogonal rectitude appropriate to the formal setting, and its entry facade completes the east boundary of the forecourt otherwise bound by the north facade of the Wight building and Forty-fifth Street. Only after the first lens slips past the plaza and begins the journey toward the garden does it relax.

As twentieth-century architects grew more interested first in democracy and eventually in the question of individuality, a few were drawn to the energy and intimacies of bodies in motion. Their architecture assumed more the character of modern dance, as if each building froze a moment in the angular frenzy of a Merce Cunningham or William Forsythe performance.

The figure of the frozen moment is not incidental, because one desire of such architecture is to convey the sense that, like each of us, a building is never complete but always in the process of becoming. When, after taking leave from the forecourt, the forms of Holl's five lenses loosen up and jitterbug down the hill, they invoke that legacy. On the facades of the lenses, lines of metal channel appear like string coursing on the otherwise mute exterior, the result of length limitations on the translucent glass planks. The architect breaks the continuation of those lines to suggest faults and fissures, further amplifying the impression that the forces shaping the lenses are very much still at work.

Actually, however, the plaza and reflecting pool take the first step of the dance when together they shift off the center axis of Wight's facade toward the Bloch. That shift refocuses attention from the original building alone to the relationship between it and its new partner, but a pivotal second step is taken when the rectangular yellow platform of De Maria's "sun" shifts even more

View to the southeast of J. C. Nichols Plaza with *One Sun / 34 Moons*, 2002, by Walter De Maria, American (b. 1935). Gilt bronze, stainless steel, reflecting pool, neon illuminated skylights, each skylight (*Moon*) 36 in. (91.44 cm) diameter; *Sun*: 17 x 486 5/16 x 405 1/4 in. (43.18 x 1,235.24 x 1,029.34 cm); Pool: 1,609 1/16 x 1,933 1/4 x 9 in. (4,087.03 x 4,910.46 x 22.86 cm). The Nelson-Atkins Museum of Art, Kansas City, Missouri. Purchase: acquired through the generosity of the Hall Family Foundation, 2002.6.

[far right] View of parking garage below *One Sun / 34 Moons*.

28

idiosyncratically toward the southeast corner of the pool. The drive of that move, directed toward the narrow gap where the Bloch and the original building meet, becomes the first strain of music that sets the forms of the lenses into motion.

If one imagines that the shifts of the pool and artwork exert a simple force on the first lens and that its walls might be able to move, one sees that the effect of that force is to push on the south end of the lens, causing it to rotate away from the orthogonal geometry established by the forecourt. Because cause and effect are so legible, an architectural purist would use a set of analytic devices termed "diagrammatic formalism" to read these dynamics. Since the metaphor of dance serves our needs perfectly well, we need not mention this more intellectual approach at all, except to point out an interesting aside.

Holl uses the various shifts on the plaza to connect the two buildings while allowing the public to glimpse the process, but the architect is at the same time engaging his formalist colleagues in a conversation about the causal legibility they champion. After the first lens, the subsequent lenses assume such manifold eccentricity that one cannot hope to account for them adequately with the techniques of formalist reading. It is as if Holl the phenomenologist is saying to his formalist colleagues that the relevance of strict legibility ends on the plaza; beyond it in the garden, the intuitive form of each lens evokes the untold influences that shape an individual personality.

De Maria's wise *One Sun / 34 Moons* adds its two cents to the conversation, of course. Amid the bliss of its too many moons,

the sun rises from the water, bulging against the strictures of the foolish geometry imposed upon it. It consents to reason for the time being, as an adult does to a child at play, knowing full well the folly of intellect's ambition to comprehend an infinitely wondrous cosmos.

But the artwork has other important jobs to do. Belonging at once to the museum's collection and to its architecture, to the old building and the new, to the underground parking structure and to the plaza, it is key to the addition's search for a new inclusiveness. It helps produce one of the most magical of its architectural effects to that end: a new roof for the museum— not a literal roof, but a phenomenal one, every bit as real, that spans the entire site from Forty-fifth Street to Cleaver II Boulevard. With this roof, the old Nelson-Atkins building, front lawn, and back gardens all disappear into a Nelson-Atkins Museum that one is always inside wherever one is—in the garage, on the plaza, in a gallery of one wing or another, or strolling in the gardens.

Much goes into the construction of such a fantastic roof, such as the cascade of translucent lenses south into the gardens where they become sculptures in the collection during the day and lamps in the museum space at night. The connection between the Bloch and the original building dissolves a strong sense of entering and exiting, as does the porosity of the Bloch's galleries to the grounds around them, so that one moves from gallery to the sculpture lawns in the spaces between the lenses in the same way that one moves from gallery to gallery. As we discover later, the very ground itself is transformed as part of the construction. Naturally, a new roof requires a new floor.

Parallel to softening the experience of entering and exiting, the Bloch relaxes the sharp distinction between art and architecture, and it is here that De Maria's sculpture makes another contribution. As we have seen and will see again, architecture old and new is always presented as part of the collection, even in the parking facility, where the light from the sculptor's thirty-four moons penetrates the sinusoidal wave-form of the ceiling to reflect the plaza and liquid depths of the pool into the garage. But the eccentric shift in the pool of De Maria's *Sun* also secures a tie between Magdalena Abakanowicz's *Standing Figures (Thirty Figures)* and George Segal's *Rush Hour* as it asks the two works if they would help the architecture by defining the limits of the forecourt. Finally, the *Sun* and *Moons* foreshadow a theme that we will soon discover to be the heart and soul of the Bloch Building and its quest for serenity and inclusiveness: light become matter.

Having plied the original building with flattery and gifts, the architect next takes a risky gambit—like the sacrifice of a pawn in chess to secure a positional advantage—in its effort to defer to its elder partner as a means of beguiling it into a more contemporary political posture. At a glance during the day, it would be easy to mistake the Bloch Building for a scattering of functional sheds, an intrusion of the ordinary into a neighborhood of beautiful homes, the rustic campus of the Kansas City Art Institute, and expressive modern and contemporary buildings, such as the Kemper Museum of Contemporary Art. In that fleeting impression, the Bloch does not belong to the local architectural context any more than Wight's monument. The difference, however, is that the extroverted 1933 building seems to come from somewhere else on a mission, as expressed in the subtitle of Wolferman's history of the museum, "Culture Comes to Kansas City." The daytime appearance of the Bloch, on the other hand, mirrors the workaday buildings of Kansas City, as if to say, "Culture has always been here, if we look for it in the right way."

To discover splendor in ever more common things, processes, and circumstances has been one of the great quests of art

throughout its history, but the pursuit obsesses much of modern and contemporary art. Very few works in the gallery dedicated to the collection from these periods remain untouched by it. Only that obsession can explain how a difficult work like John Chamberlain's *Huzzy*, which seems like it might well have been junk taken out of a trashcan, can hang next to Tom Wesselmann's slick pop painting *Still Life No. 24*, with its hilarious pack of Tareyton cigarettes and bottle of Wish-Bone Italian dressing, as if the two artworks could be spoken of in the same breath. For some of us, coming across a work like *Huzzy* can be uncomfortable; its apparent lack of artistry can make us feel vulnerable, confused, perhaps even the butt of some joke. How are we supposed to look at it, to think about it?

In the uncertainty of that moment, the museum as a contemporary institution offers a rare gift to its guest. While making no

[right] John Chamberlain, American (b. 1927). *Huzzy,* 1961. Painted and chromium-plated steel with fabric, 54 x 33 x 21 in. (137.16 x 83.82 x 53.34 cm). The Nelson-Atkins Museum of Art, Kansas City, Missouri. Gift of Mrs. Charles F. Buckwalter in memory of Charles F. Buckwalter, F64-8.

guarantees, it assures us that it just might be worth our while to let our guard down and become acquainted with the strange thing on the wall. Most important, it promises that we can do so without fear. And so some can begin to enjoy the intense beauty and celebration of process in the rust, rough edges, and bends of the painted metal and worn fabric of *Huzzy* and to grasp the connection it makes between the everyday stuff in the Wesselmann and the spontaneous actions that Jackson Pollock used to make his paintings, as seen in the example hanging just around the corner. In essence, then, today's museum is no longer an absolute authority entitled to tell us what we should think and feel, but an institution of manifest trust that mediates a priceless intimacy between total strangers: artist and viewer.

A principal part of the job of any contemporary architecture for a museum is to set the stage for that fragile encounter. It must be able to guide and direct attention without imposing its will too insistently, be generous but have an opinion—a museum is, after all, only human—while encouraging other opinions. Like the soundtrack of a film, the architecture must also shape the dramatic arc—the moods, tempos, and rhythms of intensity and repose—for each visit by innumerable persons and personalities. Compounding the complexity, an encyclopedic museum of the stature of the Nelson-Atkins contains a vast variety of art and design. It gathers under one roof (and let us not forget that that the Nelson-Atkins still has only a single roof, though its extent and location are no longer so obvious) some of the greatest achievements of old and modern masters along with lesser-known works and the adventurous and sometimes obscure, cross-your-fingers-and-pray experiments of living artists, as well as works from other cultures, other histories, other worlds.

It can be tricky to fathom the subtleties of any work of contemporary architecture in its effort to fulfill these charges, for two reasons. First, because buildings are so insinuated in the crass realities of our day-to-day life—from getting out of the rain to going to the bathroom—we bring a well-rehearsed awareness of a building's basic functions, which shapes our reaction to it over and above all other conceits. Second, like the film soundtrack, architecture can best exercise its persuasions by operating

for the most part beneath close attention; even in a museum as eye-grabbing as Frank Gehry's Guggenheim in Bilbao, the preponderance of architectural measures the building uses to choreograph the experience is barely noticed. Fortunately for us, however, an extraordinary painting in the Nelson-Atkins is perfectly suited to guide our next steps into the Bloch Building.

Tracer
Hanging in the second of the Contemporary Art Galleries is *Tracer*,[4] arguably the finest of Robert Rauschenberg's silkscreen paintings for which he won the coveted grand prize at the 1964 Venice Biennale. For this work, the artist has plucked incongruous images from books, magazines, and newspapers, transferred them to the canvas, and then stirred. We see two helicopters over

[right] Robert Rauschenberg, American (b. 1925). *Tracer,* 1963. Oil and silkscreen on canvas, 84 1/8 x 60 in. (213.68 x 152.4 cm). The Nelson-Atkins Museum of Art, Kansas City, Missouri. Purchase, F84-70.

30

Peter Paul Rubens, Flemish (1577–1640). *Venus Before a Mirror*, 1614–15. Oil on wood, 49 x 38 1/2 in. (124 x 98 cm). Collection Fürst von Liechtenstein, Vaduz, Liechtenstein.

Vietnam, a bald eagle, a pair of caged lovebirds, an excerpt from a Rubens painting, two line drawings of boxes floating around and out of the painting, and a street scene made unsettling by, if nothing else, the red that tints it.

Unlike the biting humor of the *Shuttlecocks* or the intensity of *Huzzy*, a peculiar equanimity emanates from *Tracer* despite its imagery. The space of the painting exercises no effort to lure us in, yet we and all the flotsam and jetsam in our immediate surroundings find ourselves already in it and part of it. Thus, despite first impressions, it is not a collage. Right before our very eyes and yet without our quite noticing, *Tracer*'s power of inclusion gathers its miscellany into a holistic world staged on a new kind of ground and unified by a new kind of coherence. In its own way, the Bloch Building, like the painting, also radiates a spirited calm and possesses an uncanny power of inclusion, incorporating the underground parking facility, the art, the grounds, and the original building into a new whole with the same effortless ease that has *Tracer* joining a helicopter to a seventeenth-century painting of a goddess.

Few other paintings operate so intricately at so many levels. There are the obvious slippages of meaning when, for example, aggression moves to patriotism and then on to love as symbolism passes from one bird of prey to another. But of more interest to its conversation with the Bloch Building are its formal and material means. Rauschenberg's painting is built around a remarkable catalogue of doublings: Venus is reflected in the mirror, the "helicopters" in the upper left corner are actually the same helicopter printed twice, while the film-negative source of the helicopter image appears as an almost imperceptible apparition in the lower right corner. The lovebirds are paired, the words "Coca-Cola" appear twice, the two figures in the foreground of the street scene stand in mirror symmetry, and even the apparently solitary American bald eagle reverberates as a latent figure in the white highlights of its own shoulder.

Because each image transfer brings its own space with it, *Tracer* hosts a dizzying array of spatial illusions: the street recedes deep into the canvas, the helicopter twice told hovers above Vietnam, while the same helicopter lies on the lower corner in a

space as thin as camera film; all the while, the two boxes float around in the axonometric space of geometric drawings. Yet, the cacophony of irreconcilable spaces coexists harmoniously in the familiar space of a single room. From either of the bottom corners of the painting, we can trace the line where wall meets black floor to the corner of the room as it disappears from view under a taxicab. Thus, a key ingredient of the painting's firmament is borrowed from architecture, the simple power of a room to join together everything and everyone in it, if but for an instant.

While there are light sources in each of the transferred images and a brightening in the area of the box on the left, the painting itself does not have its own light source—no illusions of illumination complement its spatial perspective. Light, shadow, white, and color are material effects of the paint and ink. The quotation of Rubens's *Venus Before a Mirror* has been screened on a white ground with blue ink swabbed quickly. The beveled glass of the mirror on Venus's left hovers in front of slashed brushstrokes, although one stroke overlaps the top edge of the glass, while the right side of the mirror disappears into a blue ether that curls around the goddess to stripe her back (or is it now her front, since a blue belly button appears where the small of her back should be?). Meanwhile, the slashing brushstrokes become even more pronounced as they move left from Venus toward the helicopters, mixing first with the blue and then with the black ink of the helicopters to enshroud them in a cloud.

Just below the helicopters, the red line drawing of a box floats free of gravity—as an arrow tells us. Paint, continuing to thicken, washes under the box and just laps over its lower edge before encroaching on the eagle, turbulently churning up more black ink as it begins to encircle the bird in a vortex whose strokes end in heavy daubs of paint. If we scan to this same vortex starting instead from the room's floor at the lower left corner, what we see is white paint erupting from the room's wall to capture the eagle in a violent cartouche. Under the spell of the painting's alchemy, light become visceral matter has congealed into a second spatial ground.

When that second ground encounters the New York street scene screened in red, things get interesting. The largest single image in work, it depicts a pedestrian in the foreground waiting for a taxicab to clear an intersection, a hard-hatted construction worker to his right, and the street's building fronts receding into deep perspective from the corner, where a cafeteria sign is circled in white. The heavy white strokes of paint at the bottom of the eagle spill into the top of the scene, thrusting the head of the waiting pedestrian toward us. Just to his right, a ghostly white rectangle pulls the wheel and quarter panel of the taxi out of the street scene even closer to us than the pedestrian and makes the rectangle to its left—a chimera of body, cab, and ink—almost seem like a chest of drawers, the cab's blurred door medallions its top drawer handles.

So, *Tracer* is a magical room, and what wizardries we see it perform. Follow the left wall up from the floor and it soars beyond ideas and the disturbing events of the world into the heavens; follow the right wall up, and find a Rubens hanging on it. This is not just any room, then, but a gallery. The original Rubens painting, *Venus at Her Mirror*, has been cropped tightly, bringing the viewer in close. *Tracer's* corner perspective places the Venus farther away on the wall of the gallery, at mid-distance. The inscrutable dashed line across her bottom has cut away the red upholstered chair upon which the she sat for four centuries and replaces it with another red piece of furniture in the gallery—the buildings of the street scene, on which she now sits. The painting, then, seems to say that the whole world is an art gallery, with every person, thing, and event in it a part of its collection. Have we not already heard something like that before? "All the world's a stage,/And all the men and women merely players;/They have their exits and their entrances,/And one man in his time plays many parts…" But then, whether as a stage or a gallery, architecture has always shaped our lives at levels that none of us truly comprehend.

There are three clues, then, that *Tracer* offers to its inclusiveness and edgy composure: doubling, a new kind of ground, and light as matter. We have only to check the Bloch Building for its versions of each of these clues to see what role in the architecture it might play.

Doubling

Since at least the late fourteenth century, painting has been likened to a view through a window. This tenacious analogy is credited, among other things, with the discovery of perspective, and some of the most sophisticated developments in architecture continue to derive from it. Steven Holl's Y House in the Catskill Mountains, for example, replaces the predictable large picture window looking out on a spectacular view with a compound window-wall consisting of eight panes of various sizes of rectangular glass arranged to resemble a late Mondrian painting. Thus, every time the client looks out on "nature" he sees a "painting." Like much of Holl's work, the experiment straddles the conceptual and the phenomenological, suggesting that for some at least, art has today become more authentic than nature.

The analogy thrives inside the Bloch Building, where the ubiquitous translucent glass and milk-white walls hold the focal length of the eye to a mid-distance, quietly establishing the limits of a snug zone to amplify the presence of the art and encourage close attention. Two circumstances occasion more distant views and allow attention to relax. First, interior vistas from the lobby, along the spine, and in the ceiling reveals between galleries invite eye and mind to wander to the pleasures of the voluptuous curves, folded walls, and small-scale details such as the twisted struts of the handrails. Second, intermittent zones of transparent glass capture views and frame them as borrowed art, whether they are of the neighborhood houses, the streetscape, or the sculpture park. There are two variations on the theme that merit special mention. First, in the lower lobby, we encounter the limestone wall and three doors of the old entrance to the east wing that now connect the original building to the Bloch to form one continuous museum. Though obviously not transparent glass, the abrupt presence of the wall signaled by the change in materiality produces the same transparency effect. Again, the Bloch Building makes its colleague both partner and art. Certainly, the depictions of Henry Wadsworth Longfellow's *Hiawatha* in the twenty-four cast bronze panels of the 1933 doors have never been so underscored.

The transparent wall that cleaves the Noguchi gallery and its courtyard serves less to borrow the landscape as a painting than

to join the space of the gallery to the sculpture park. It is a
poignant episode; the stone-lined catch for the spill water of the
fountain passes under the glass wall and continues to the courtyard. The courtyard meanwhile is surfaced in the same granite
pavers as the gallery, though in a different pattern and texture—
polished in the gallery, rough in the courtyard. Just beyond the
glass, the stones bridge a small "stream" of grass before reaching
the court. The play of imprecise symmetries makes the glass both
window and mirror, merging the world of the garden and world
of introspection into the same reality.

Many architects of other contemporary museums have used
transparency similarly to frame views, but in one instance at
least, Holl uses the window/painting relationship to a more radical end, one that brings us back to *Tracer*. If we take a second
look at Rauschenberg's *Venus*, we notice that while her face in
the glass looks straight at us, her gaze tinged with eroticism, the
goddess herself appears actually to look away, as if out of a window or perhaps at the doubled image of the helicopter, but in
either case in the fixed way one might contemplate a view or art.
Since we know she is at her mirror simply to see herself, the cir-
cuitous pathway of her gaze in the painting draws a marvelous
map of the twists through the world taken in the course of self-
reflection. The Bloch Building reenacts that strange pathway

almost literally, doubles it, and then goes back in time and doubles it yet again before it happened in the first place.

However you enter the museum, whether from the old building, the parking facility, or through the forecourt doors, your first
encounter with art in the new building is to see other visitors
viewing paintings and sculpture as you look at them through the
glass doors of the Contemporary Art galleries, where Willem de
Kooning's *Woman IV*, *Huzzy*, *Tracer*, and Robert Arneson's *Pablo
Ruiz with Itch*, along with scores of other famously ill-mannered
misfits, stand around and hang out. You notice your own reflection in the glass against the backdrop of art as you walk in,
chuckle at the equation, then light down the stairs. After about
ten minutes in the gallery, you glance back out through the glass
only to see another visitor looking in at you. In that split second,
you realize that the lobby scene you now see framed by the glass
entry might as well be hanging on the wall in the gallery, and,
come to think of it, it *is* hanging on the wall in the gallery, and,
finally, that the gallery scene the viewer in the lobby now sees is
actually the first work of art he sees, turning you into the same
work of art you just now turned your counterpart into, and that
the person looking at you was you ten minutes ago and will be
you again in just a few more minutes.

33

A New Ground

It is not hard to tell that something is afoot with the ground of the Holl expansion, something unusual. The original building takes command of the land with the full weight of its authority. Its giant Ionic columns, like sentries forever at attention, assert the resolve of its foothold as its temple staircases elevate the visitor from the vulgarities of the everyday to the nobility of its lofty domain. But the Bloch Building's light-berg lenses drift afloat, bobbing amid swells of lawn gently lapping at their sides. At the south end of the first lens just before the stairs, we catch one swell lifting the paving from beneath our feet to a crest; beneath it a facet of the lens resurfaces. Old building and new are as "stone and feather," an epithet meant not only to suggest differences in temperament but also to recall Galileo's demonstration that when summoned by the deeper truth of gravity, even two natures so very different become the same.

Place, ground, and land seem more or less synonymous, but for certain disciplines, like politics, law, and architecture, each of these and related concepts carry crucial distinctions. According to phenomenology, we have a native relationship to place that precedes all identities and laws that we later learn, and place is rooted in the ground. Yet, it is land on which we live out our lives; land names our collective and individual relations to the ground as effects of a constellation of laws and social practices. Ground and land are distinct yet inextricable; if we think of homeland or landlord, we think of feelings of patriotism, or just being at home. While we regularly seek to transform place by changing the land, say, with new names or laws, the expansion seeks to transform the place of the Nelson-Atkins Museum by changing its ground.

With modern architecture's urge to democracy came perhaps its greatest experiment: to renovate profoundly the traditional relationship between building and ground. Recognizing classical architecture's participation in a bond between power and land that dates from feudal times, modern architecture sought the means to break that bond. Le Corbusier, for example, lifted his buildings into the air to return the land to free ground. If his idea today seems naive, it and others like it set into motion a

As you continue through the galleries, should you visit the small conference room south of the upstairs library in the first lens, or the meeting room above the contemporary gallery in the second lens, you will notice picture windows with glorious views of the streetscape and grounds. But now you will also notice that the large window in the next lens faces back at you. If perchance someone is in that window, you will again be looking at yourself through the eyes of another.

What you will not realize, until a subsequent visit finds you entering the Bloch Building from the fountain forecourt, is that the addition has already set this journey of self-reflection through art into motion, because the glass forecourt entry is actually the first of these paintings with you in it. Just above the two doors that rotate into the first lens, a fissure in the skin of the lens divides the lobby space visible through the long glass wall into two sections. To the left, you see a relaxed arrangement of the café and other customary accoutrements of a back lobby. On the other hand, to the right is something quite different. An uninterrupted wash of translucent interior glass on the rear wall thins the space of the front lobby as seen from the forecourt into a minimalist canvas, cut full-length by the diagonal of the open staircase. Just behind the staircase begins the ramp down to the galleries. So, as you approach the doors, you see an oddly familiar painting of bodies ascending and descending a staircase (though not nude), and a moment later the painting includes you.

century of efforts to invent more poetic and psychological means by which architecture might truly disentangle the building from land as the exercise of power.

For example, where Wight's building greets the arrival of the visitor with great aplomb, the Bloch Building stages no such ceremony. We do not enter the Bloch Building so much as find a footpath into it from here or there, from the original building, the parking facility, the south gardens, even in passing from the sidewalk along Rockhill Road. We simply cross a threshold—always on grade—into an ethereal space where vaults, cusps, and folds sculpt a ceiling that filters light like a coppice at dawn. In contrast to the interior splendor of the original building, inside the Bloch it is easy to forget that we are in an important civic institution. Its space encourages us to amble around—up, down, through the galleries, out to the sculpture park and back in again.

The garden spaces between the lenses are so important to the architecture that it is better to consider them open-air galleries, even though, like the gallery room of *Tracer,* they lack not only a ceiling but also two walls. Doubling the interior galleries, these exterior rooms amplify the sense that the sculptures contained in them, and by extension all of the outdoor sculptures, are "in" the museum. At the same time, linked to the interior galleries as way stations on a meandering path, they blur the distinction between floor and ground, lightening the mood and relaxing the decorum inside.

The architect's dedication to the meander reaches a literal extreme between the second and third lenses, where the paved walkway zigzags back and forth like the notorious convolutions of its namesake, the Maeander River. One suspects Holl imagines here some furtive hops through the shrubs to spice the walk with a dash of misbehavior.

Farther on, between the fourth and fifth lenses, a quieting occurs on a simple lawn floor, where two sculptures whisper about a meander of their own. Whether of great consequence or none at all, some coincidences possess such serendipity that the soul cannot accept them as chance though the mind insists otherwise; these we call fate. The appearance together just here of Tony Cragg's *Ferryman* and *Turbo* is such a happenstance. The story of the two sculptures coming to the Nelson-Atkins Museum is a parable in miniature of the best ambitions of the Bloch, not to mention incontrovertible proof that magic happens.

Conceived years apart, *Ferryman* and *Turbo* each belong to a different series by the artist, and one has little to do with the other except for a family resemblance. The two works embarked from the studio on separate journeys but somehow found themselves together in the gallery of Cragg's New York dealer, Marian Goodman, who temporarily lent them to a public art project that placed them at one of the entrances to Central Park. There they stood, two strangers glancing awkwardly at each other, aware that in the eyes of passersby accidental proximity and family name made them appear a couple. Today, having meandered around the world, they have finally settled together in a garden gallery, as a couple made for each other. So charmingly do they twin the relationship between the addition and the original building that is it hard not to believe that they were commissioned for the purpose.

Playing the role of the original building stands the opaque, topsy *Turbo*, once the very image of power and stalwart industrial will, now a lovable relic of a great history struggling valiantly but in vain to stay in motion and to resist the wear and tear of time on its body, its dignity, and its way of being in the world. Playing the Bloch Building is the porous and wiggly *Ferryman* who basks in change—a wisp to *Turbo's* will. Translucent during the day, *Ferryman* glows at night as the light from the Bloch spills through its pores.

It is nigh impossible to interpret *Ferryman*; certainly its name gives little clue. Trying to find in it anything to do with Charon the ferryman of Greek mythology is an exercise in befuddlement. One gets no help either from its form, which belongs to a kind of mathematical oddity called a Klein bottle, a sort of three-dimensional Moebius strip. To be honest, other than the sheer pleasure of getting lost in it, one of the most enjoyable things about *Ferryman* is the distress it causes professional art critics, who struggle to offer convincing interpretations—one after another see in it the whole universe, the structure of matter, a cat stretching, two people making love, and dozens of other free associations. No holy smoke yet, but it should not be too long. The artist offers a pretty good clue:

> There are obvious objects such as chairs or tables. Yet, "in between," other objects could exist... For instance, you know what a pig looks like. And, you know what an elephant looks like. But, you don't know what a "Piggy-Phant" looks like... And, if you met it in the park you'd be afraid! A "Piggy-Phant" would be a "new reality." This is what a sculptor is doing—looking for "Piggy-Phants."[5]

But the buildings and these works reflect each other at another level. For the better part of his career and across an unbelievable assortment of sculptural experiments, Cragg has been guided by a compulsion to synthesize in as many ways as imaginable two great traditions of sculpture's history that by the 1960s had come to oppose each other: figure and field.[6]

Sculpture and figure were for centuries, even millennia, almost synonymous. People all over the world have fallen under the spell of the aura of the solitary sculptural figure, whether representational or abstract. It is the stuff not only of art, but of archaeology, history, and religion, and we need only walk for a while among the Nelson-Atkins's collection of Henry Moores to be reminded of this. The roots of sculptural fields are also ancient, as Stonehenge and the buried terra-cotta warriors in Xian, China, bring to mind. By the 1960s, however, the time-honored predisposition toward the figure had so shifted to the field that influential artists and critics considered the figural

tradition to have all but exhausted its creative possibilities. Sculpture as field, it was thought, broke free from the self-orientation of the figure to engage the more complex manifold that constituted modernity's social, political, and formal space.

In his early works, Cragg started with a field, which he then drew toward a unified figure. Typically, he might gather large numbers of familiar objects—plastic toys, combs, cups, plates—and compose these into large, easy-to-recognize two-dimensional figures, such as a crescent moon, a painter's palette, or a silhouette of a person. No matter how one paid attention to one of these works, whether looking closely at its individual elements or taking in its overall composition, one recognized something in its own right, a toy shovel or bubble blower, never a simplified part subordinated to a larger whole. The ever whimsical quality of both the colorful elements and the overall figure also countered the leaden solemnity that sculpture had accrued over centuries, and a fresh door opened for the discipline. Works like these by Cragg and other artists gave sculpture a powerful vocabulary with which to imagine new affiliations between one and many as metaphors for connections between the individual and the collective. Eventually, Cragg's assemblies began to consolidate into denser accumulations—a stack of bottles or crockery, for example. *Turbo* and *Ferryman* may seem to return to the traditional sculptural figure, but are more intriguing when we understand them as continuations of the artist's process of compressing whimsical fields into figures.

In keeping with its strict sense of order, neoclassical architecture is the study par excellence in the subordination of the part to the whole at every conceivable level of detail, from the importance of proportions to the hierarchical ordering of the architectural elements of the massing and the plans, to the use of ornamentation and decor. If *Turbo* is less disciplined than the Wight building, it shows strong traces of neoclassical order in its stacking of disks from small to medium to large and back in mirror symmetry. Neither *Ferryman* nor the Bloch Building obeys such rules, but more important, each is more concerned than its counterpart with an unassuming participation in a field than with the assertion of a figure. Perhaps the difficulty that critics have had thus far in interpreting *Ferryman* has been caused by the fact that, still in the thrall of old habits, they think the most important thing about the work is the organic metal form, when, all along, its been about the holes.

Taking advantage of the fact that architecture does not only depict relationships between one and many, but actually stages them, the Bloch is able to go *Ferryman* one better in its particular proposition about fields, inclusiveness, and imagining new connections between individual and collective. But to do so, it must take a substantial architectural risk.

Because of its porosity and informality, departing the fourth lens for the sculpture park brings no denouement, no satisfying sense of conclusion. Classical architects, keenly aware of the effect of their building's relationship to land and power, used it to craft endings with an operatic touch. With the last step off Wight's grand staircase into the sculpture park terraces, the weight of the building's protocol begins to lift from our shoulders, and a giddy feeling of liberation overtakes us as we move farther into the gardens. Palaces, villas, and their counterparts in every country around the world have developed that transition into a cornucopia of creative processionals and garden types to and from the building, and it is no accident that nineteenth-century literature is so rich with romantic trysts in manor gardens. The Bloch Building does not take leave because it seeks to join us as a companion presence in our wanderings away from its interior, intrinsic to the edge-less extent of its new ground. If by the time we leave, the building has not already shed all sense of control over us to become, in a sense, one of us or part of us, it risks orchestrating a disappointing conclusion.

The freedom sought by the Bloch Building, then, is not just the momentary license that obtains from the recess of embodied authority, but an abiding freedom of the spirit that we can carry with us wherever we go. Yet, for the Bloch to take such a risk and aspire to attain such intimacy with us is not just a matter of how free it might make us feel. If the Bloch's new ground can conjure such a compelling equivalence, then something more miraculous can occur. After all, the five lenses we see are not individual pavilions but manifestations of one

building that we cannot see. The new ground of the Nelson-Atkins forged by the Bloch extends the manifestations beyond the five lenses to include the original building and the garden sculptures as other kinds of lenses that join into a unity that we need never see. As are we.

Light Matters

For all the achievements of the new addition, any claim it makes for immortality will turn on the night, when the Bloch Building is made of light, like other buildings are made of limestone or brick. It glows but the light does not move, arrested in such perfect stillness that it has time to acquire stiffness, tangibility, and weight and sink into the ground. In winter when the surrounding trees are bare, the light incorporates them as if to become a colossal gelatin-silver print or perhaps a Chinese handscroll. As one approaches, the apparition spellbinds, intensifying rather than weakening; one begins to hear it and feel its coolness. Its appeal is so immediate and complete that it is difficult to fathom that this light-become-matter is Steven Holl's most daring experiment with a new authenticity, and his most precarious.

The vulnerabilities are patently obvious. As an illusion of material and technology, it is subject to the all too familiar life cycle of engineered magic. Electricity is not free, and the Bloch Building will require long-term maintenance and cleaning. Even with the best of care it will weather and age, while new breakthroughs will enable more spectacular trickery. So we will become inured, as we did with Gothic cathedrals, perspective, and moon landings. But these are results of the properties of matter itself, and the history of art and architecture are testimony to the power of authenticity not just to survive the exposures of matter but also to spring from them.

"One-of-a-kind" is the name we give to art's obstinacy against such degradations, but the construction techniques used by Holl and McVoy are easy to imitate, so we will see similar buildings cropping up everywhere, all the more because of the addition's success. However certain we feel that the total achievement of its architecture is more than sufficient to elevate this work to a one-of-a-kind, in truth only time can tell.

But the most controversial effect of the Bloch Building's glowing exterior is surely its complicity with a pervasive and increasingly decried feature of our contemporary cities, night lighting. Scientists despair and sociologists warn of dire consequences that attend the pending extinction of night. Anyone of a phenomenological bent must be keenly aware of the depth that the dark night is ingrained in our aboriginal being. We know from the uncanny stillness of its glow and the dedication to shadow of its chiaroscuro that great care has been taken to guarantee that the Bloch does not wound the night. Nevertheless, for an architect of Holl's disposition to challenge darkness must give us pause.

Now, the mundane reality is that even if the lenses were permanently switched off, Holl and McVoy have secured a place for the Nelson-Atkins among museums renowned for the use of light. Thanks to science and engineering, architects today know more about light and have more power to control it than ever before in history. This knowledge includes the spectral and scattering effects of various glasses, plastics, and surface finishes, computer-control shading devices, and advanced artificial lighting systems that allow the color temperature—the red or blue bias of the light—to be tuned much as one increases the treble or bass in a stereo. Less obvious but no less valuable is the ability of engineers to enable the architect to place windows, lunettes, slots, and other strategic light apertures in roofs and walls without compromising structural integrity.

But choreographing the play of light inside a museum is not a science; it is an art and like any art, its practitioners vary in their talents and personalities, as do their results. Louis Kahn launched our golden age of museum light in 1972 with the opening of his Kimbell Art Museum in Fort Worth, Texas, not because of its extraordinary engineering or bland neutrality, but rather because of its distinct architectural character, its reserve and serenity. For all it owes the Kimbell, the Bloch is a different creature.

Indeed, despite the popular misconception of "the white box" there is no such thing as an ideal neutrality of light and form for a museum; not even architects and museum directors whose tastes lean toward white boxes believe that. Nor, for that matter, is there even such a thing as natural light. We are aware of a

painter's predilection for north light, thinking rightly of the value its even luminosity pays throughout the day. We may be less aware that painters also relish the fact that north light is fickle, changing colors a little with each chance reflection and so animating the paint on the canvas with endless fidgets of hue and overtone. Which, then, is the natural light, south or north?

Long before sunlight passes through a pane of glass and glances off a facing wall, it is chosen by the building, which then colors, filters, dims, shapes, and otherwise manipulates it. A building thus recapitulates the processes Earth herself uses to calm the unbearable insults hurled at us by the Sun into warmth and daylight. And even these, without further mitigation, remain too noxious to endure full measure. It would be more accurate to say that each building uniquely stirs the brute materiality of sunlight into a poignant potion that we call Natural Light.

Of course, architecture cannot claim exclusive license to blend this infusion. Urban and landscape designers, for example, each mix their own cocktails of natural light, from wholesale and quotidian to rare and intimate. But as poets, artists, and filmmakers attest, architecture can craft exquisite achievements in the stuff. From inspiring shafts to shimmering shadows to hypnotic washes, architecture's Natural Light whispers directly into our soul. We offer it no resistance as it rouses in us divine awe or abject horror, lascivious sensuality or transcendent repose at a whim.

Architecture's powers with light border on the mystical; a building can, for example, transform any profane source into Natural Light. What else can in the time it takes to draw a breath detect a pair of headlights moving down a road at night, capture its beams and the tree shadows they subtend; stretch, reflect, refract, and double these, blend in more ingredients — silhouettes of furniture, dancing shadows of drapes and blinds— and then project this ghostly ballet onto a bedroom wall? We have all been enthralled by these night-light visitations. They last but seconds by the clock, but they stretch time into concrete substantiations of Henri Bergson's *duration.*

In this sense a museum is a special optical instrument akin in many ways to those nineteenth-century microscopes, telescopes, and the like, whose sculptural form and impeccable crafting still earn our admiration, though their true measure rests even today on the achievements of their lenses. But where these instruments transform their source light into scientific images, buildings transform source light into something entirely different, into moods and evocations and atmosphere.

As we abandon a naive notion of natural light, then, we should reaffirm it as a constructed phenomenon no less real, no less essential, no less transcendent. As a construction, Natural Light carries all of the histories intrinsic to any construction, histories of time and place, of course, but also of materials and technology, culture, economics, sociology, and politics. One can see this unfold as the evolution of the construction of holy light, for example, from the phallic shaft at the Pantheon to the colored spray at Chartres to the chthonic tones at Ronchamp to the equanimous wash of pale in Jorn Utzon's Church at Bagsvaerd, another of the Bloch's predecessors. Thus Natural Light itself is a topic for research into new authenticities—a topic Steven Holl has made his life's study.

Holl names the five structures that dance across the site "lenses" to stir us from our habitual expectations of a building and to cue us to the new experiences and thoughts he wants the architecture addition to engender. Indelibly linked to vision, the notion of a lens calls attention to the fact that the structures we see are not—despite appearances—independent pavilions but exaggerated clerestories of a single building that capture light and transmit it to the galleries below; in that sense, the term *lens* is perhaps not so far afield after all. The word reminds us, too, that art is never a practice of representation, but is itself a particular lens through which we see irreproducible and original views of life. But most of all, the term speaks to the building's obsession with light, which is at work in myriad subtle ways at every moment of the day, in every location and at every scale, nudging us sotto voce toward the art we have come to see.

When we enter the first lens, for example, so many pleasures vie for our interest that it is unlikely we will pay much attention to the large plaster wall, though radiant sprites glint across a paler shade of light on its impenetrable surface as its lustrous finish reflects back the translucency and transparency of the exterior glass. This wall is the kind of thing we are likely to take for granted, not realizing the amount of energy expended to make it just so. To achieve the finish and large seamless expanse of area required a plastering technique called hard-troweling, which demands that the entire wall be completed in one application before the plaster dries, using a uniform stroke. To prepare, the architects and the team of some fifteen plasterers together studied the arm motion that best yielded the desired finish, and then held practice sessions on mock walls to coordinate the final application.

Later, as we walk through the galleries, if Neil Welliver's painting *Late Squall* happens to catch our attention and we find something oddly familiar about it, it may be that, like the plaster wall, our eye cannot penetrate the even tone of the painting's surface and its snowflakes' glisten. But then, perhaps it is no coincidence. To achieve those effects, Welliver built his paintings like the plasterers built the wall, adding wet paint to wet and finishing each painting in one session, "direct," in the lingo of the discipline.

As in *Tracer*, light and white and paint and wall all come to life as one fantastic protean organism, a living ephemera that haunts the galleries of the Bloch to extraordinary end. Using it, the gifted curators and installers of the Nelson-Atkins conjure their own miracles. Pink, translucent light flows like skim milk from the wall into the canvas of Agnes Martin's *White Flower II*, soaking around its gray bands and atop its cream ones, exhibiting the artist's genius for constructing a wholly original painterly space as few museums have ever done. Yet right next to it, light recedes from the harsh white of Ellsworth Kelly's painting *White Black* to become a shadow of its light, if such a thing might be imagined. Similar effects happen many times over throughout the galleries and collections, and far more often than not to good end. But not always; some may agree, for example, that the LeWitt sculptures are not as well served. The multiple-source reflected light in the gallery butts into the artwork's internal play between mathematical hard-edge and op reverberation to muddy it a bit. No one singer can sing every song well, fortunately.

The stroke of ingenuity that enables so many of the Bloch Building's interior effects is the triple duty performed by those elements in the building the architects call the "breathing" or "fluttering" Ts. These thick masts camouflage structure, ductwork, and electrical service, unfettering the outer walls to enable the translucency, and they hoist the network of light scoops that reflect the sunlight from the lenses into the galleries along manifold gradients and ray paths. The Ts intersect large areas excised from the ceilings to form luminous voids that add pictorial interest and plasticity to the space while further kneading the light. Many of the scoops assume a form that faintly echoes the vaults of Romanesque cathedrals. These add a dash of solemnity to temper the informal atmosphere produced when the other scoops distort into warps and facets and branch into one another to weave the ceiling into a surreal garden arbor.

More than an optical instrument, then, the Bloch Building is a light-manufacturing factory. Whether it originated from the sun or an electric light fixture, before any single photon is allowed to leave the Bloch for someone's eye—inside the galleries or out—it has been processed and reprocessed: bounced, bent, stretched, and filtered by physics, educated by history, groomed by psychology, and scented by poetry. This new light of the Bloch is its radical claim for a new authenticity

But then, what about the night? Like every city these days, Kansas City is awash in typical night lighting: cars, signs, streetlights, sidewalk lamps in Art Deco lampposts, architectural spotlighting, and cosmetic highlighting. In addition, it boasts its own quirkier lights; during the winter holiday season, the entire fourteen square blocks of the Plaza shopping district is decked out in strings of multicolored Christmas lights. Nothing, however, quite compares to Frank Lloyd Wright's contribution to Kansas City's evening glory, the great steeple of light that blasts into the heavens through the roof of the Community Christian Church in midtown.[7]

The dilemma is simple to articulate and presents a classic scenario for both critical and phenomenological speculation on the potential consequences for architecture. Because of night lighting, cities are safer and more active, pleasant places to be, and buildings lit at night add drama and spectacle to skyline and streetscape alike. In some version, it is here to stay. But the escalation of urban night lighting contributes on several fronts to real ecological problems that adversely affect us all—not just astronomers.

For Holl the general issue must stand on a conjecture that we, today's city dwellers, have become a kind of being for whom light at night is no longer just a convenience, but a basic element of our world. The specifically architectural issue derives from the unfortunate fact that, popularity notwithstanding, current practices of architectural night lighting—all of which are merely copied from stage lighting—count among the most inauthentic of architectural effects, crass dispiriting display and nothing more.

As its response, the Bloch Building conjures a new light that belongs to architecture, speaks to the soul, and savors the night.

Notes

1. Throughout this essay, the theme of inclusiveness will recur, and in that spirit let us be reminded that the name "Steven Holl" herein refers not just to an architect, but to a collaboration between a firm and a team assembled to complete the building that includes engineers, consultants, associate architects, landscape architects, and construction personnel—all indispensable to the work. In terms of the design, the fundamental contribution of project architect and partner-in-charge Chris McVoy, the work's co-principal architect, must be singled out.

2. Kristie C. Wolferman, *The Nelson-Atkins Museum of Art: Culture Comes to Kansas City* (Columbia, MO: University of Missouri Press, 1993), pp. 122–32.

   This essay is deeply indebted to Chief Curator Deborah Emont Scott for her guidance on the collection and the museum's history. Among her many acts of generosity was to provide this delightful book, from which most of the stories and facts regarding the architecture of the original building herein have been taken.

   Some of the tales that its author narrates of the early beginnings of the Museum border on the miraculous, such as the fact the prestigious permanent collection covering Oriental, European, and American fine and decorative arts with which the Museum opened in 1933 was acquired entirely from scratch in just three scant years. It is hard to imagine the combination of will, audacity, scholarship, management, logistics, energy, and wealth it took to accomplish such a feat, not to mention the sheer luck: the curators were spending their generous budget just at the moment that the world was suffering one of it worst depressions. Wolferman's account of this amazing episode is made all the more delicious by the tidbits of controversy and intrigue she adds: "Meanwhile, the [*Kansas City*] *Post* continued to raise doubts about the quality and authenticity of the new purchases. At one point, the *Post* tried to convince its readers that the trustees had paid a ring of crooks more than $1 million for fake art."

3. The dramatic staging of the sculpture, also known as the *Winged Victory*, by the architecture produces the inescapable effect of convincing everyone that it is the most important of masterpieces. The placement of the sculpture is notorious because it enables the work to look down on an approaching viewer, in keeping with the tradition of Roman sculpture. The optimum view of the *Nike,* a Greek sculpture, is on the same level as the visitor, at a 45-degree angle. The work depicts a goddess on a ship's prow, a scene a viewer would expect to see from the side, and if you really want to see the miracle of the sculpture, when her stone fabric becomes weightless and ripples in the wind, you must press your back as far into the corner of the staircase platform wall as you can. In other words, to achieve the spectacular hyperbole in its presentation of the work, the architecture violently subverts the artwork itself.

4. The indeterminacy of Venus's stare in *Tracer* as compared to the activity in the painting's four corners calls attention to the genius, ineptitude, psychology, and dumb luck found in any good work of art, including the Bloch Building. The pictorial calculations behind Rauschenberg's dissection of the Rubens are truly remarkable. In the original, Cupid holds up a hand mirror mounted in a heavy wood frame, as an African handmaiden stands to Venus's right combing her hair. Formally, the goddess's view terminates at Cupid's left hand, a vertex of a triangle that confines the zone of attention (the other vertices are her eye and his right shoulder). Rauschenberg cuts out Cupid, the wood frame of the mirror, and everything else to the left and above the bevel of mirror glass to allow Venus's gaze to reach out toward the helicopters, the mirror to float, and the white cloud of paint to wash into blue ether.

   His handling of the corners is something else. He leaves intact the figure of the African handmaiden on the right, barely visible in the transfer (look for the white dots of her bead necklace just above the bottom line of the floating box). Formally, the handmaiden held the upper right corner of the Rubens, and probably was intended to do the same for *Tracer*, but the transfers of it and the helicopter negative in the lower right corner misalign, warping into the field to leave raw canvas in both corners.

   At the top, the artist has painted a geometric half-box, recapturing the head of the handmaiden to resolve the corner brilliantly. At the bottom he tries to fix the corner by extending the diagonal of the black floor with an afterthought daub of black overpainting, but does not quite get it to line up with the diagonal exactly. Still, his clumsiness yields a satisfying irresolution to the corner that makes the relationship between the pictorial field, the perspectival space, and the canvas itself all the more complex.

   Now, one might attribute these corner effects to the artist's plans, but given the resolve of the other two corners, it seems more likely that both were lucky recoveries from accidents, his stock-in-trade. Yet many of Rauschenberg's transfer paintings of 1963–64 show a struggle at the corners whose character is markedly different from the swaggering spontaneity with which he approaches the main canvas, more fidgety and insecure.

   Perhaps the corner dramas are not so surprising. After leaving the Kansas City Art Institute (across the street from the Nelson-Atkins), the artist landed at Black Mountain College to study painting with the disciplined and methodical Bauhaus formalist Josef Albers. To say the least, the two got on each other's nerves; while crediting Albers as his most influential teacher, Rauschenberg also describes his lifelong compulsion to do exactly the reverse of everything his teacher stood for. The corner is a classical problem in painting, and perhaps no other painter in history has given as much consideration to it as Albers, whose magnum opus, *Homage to the Square* included over one thousand works and spanned twenty-five years.

5. See http://parisvoice.com/03/apr/html/art/art.cfm.

6. See, for example, Rosalind Krauss' seminal essay "Sculpture in the Expanded Field," *October* 8 (Spring 1979), pp. 30-44. See also http://orchid.cs.uiuc.edu/people/adamczyk/pvss/readings/Krauss.pdf.

7. Although the steeple of light was part of Wright's 1940 proposal, it was not realized until 1994.

Sketches

Steven Holl

We began our sketches for The Nelson-Atkins Museum of Art in April 1999. The rewards of eight years of work, and countless dedicated hours by many individuals, are now tangible but still intangible. The energy of the artworks within is like the music that fills a new concert hall. Like the acoustic anticipation of a new concert hall, our visual anticipation of the artworks yields most exciting rewards of the interiors. Even more important for architecture than exterior iconic form is the interior space defined.

What follows is a chronological selection of texts written over the period of the expansion project, 1999–2007.

1999

In the original design competition, there was a strong mind-set for building the new addition against the existing building to the north. When I first visited the site, the feeling of the landscape and the integrity of the original 1933 building impressed me. I felt the new addition could fuse with the landscape, offer new views out into the south gardens, and connect to the existing building without blocking off the north facade. In other words, the integrity of the original architecture would be preserved and restored while the new addition would merge with the landscape.

Original Building	New (in Complementary Contrast)
Opaque	Transparent
Heavy	Light
Hermetic	Meshing
Inward views	Views to landscape
Bounded	Unbounded
Directed circulation	Open circulation
Single mass	Transparent lenses

Zhou Chen, Chinese (1455–1536).
The North Sea (section), Ming Dynasty (1368–1644). Handscroll: ink and light color on silk, 11 1/8 x 53 1/2 in. (28.25 x 135.89 cm).
The Nelson-Atkins Museum of Art, Kansas City, Missouri. Purchase: Nelson Trust, 58-55.

The first time that I spent several hours viewing the Museum's collection was in the spring of 1999. I had just arrived from Hiva Hoa in the French Polynesian Islands, where my wife, the artist Solange Fabião, was making a film sited at the 1903 grave marker of the painter Paul Gauguin. I was incredibly excited to see in the Nelson-Atkins collection a superb example of Gauguin's Tahiti work in *Faaturuma (Melancholic)*, also called *The Dreamer*, of 1891. Having just been in his former studio in the Marquesas Islands, the modest circumstances of the end of his life seemed to be magnified by the look in the eyes of "the Dreamer." Gauguin's freedom and use of brilliant color juxtapositions seem to lift the whole work out of melancholy. It is this spiritual tenuousness that seems so intense in this particular painting.

A strong relationship between the architectural concept and the Museum's important Asian art holdings is illustrated by works in the permanent collection such as *Verdant Mountains* (12th century) by Jiang Shen and *The North Sea* (16th century) by Zhou Chen, which demonstrate the timeless merging of art, architecture, and landscape. The new addition celebrates this fusion with the new Isamu Noguchi Sculpture Court, setting a binding connection to the existing Kansas City Sculpture Park.

—*The Nelson-Atkins Museum of Art Member Magazine*

2000

The Stone and the Feather (landscape into architecture)
The idea of complementary contrast drove our design for an addition to The Nelson-Atkins Museum of Art, a classical stone temple and surrounding landscape. The addition is not an object: we envisioned a new paradigm fusing landscape and architecture. In contrast to the stone building, the new light-weight architecture of glass lenses is scattered about the landscape, framing sculpture gardens. The visitor's experience will be newly charged with full and partial views of landscape: sequences of shifting perspectives open to spaces where landscape merges with architecture. The movement of the body as it crosses through overlapping perspectives, through the landscape, and the free movement threaded between the light-gathering lenses of the new addition are the elemental connections between ourselves and architecture.

— *Parallax,* Princeton Architectural Press, 2000

2002

The Bloch Building at the Nelson-Atkins Museum is horizontal but it's moving down; the section gently, gently drops. This goes 840 feet, like a 70-story skyscraper lying down in the grass and you're walking through it. We studied perspectives at every shift and change as well as every drop. And any time we drop a floor to another floor we never raise that more than 3 feet, or 3.5 feet, so when we are standing in *this* space, and *that* space is a little higher, we can see across the floor of *that* space. That draws you through. You never block the spatial overlap by shifting the floor too far. You always have the continuity of one space overlapping another one. If you don't work it out in perspectives or in your brain ahead of time, it doesn't work; if you just try to draw a bunch of plans or sections and don't think about spatial overlap, it doesn't work. And it's also something that's very hard to convey in photographs. You really need to move through it with your body. Only the people who visit the Nelson-Atkins and actually go down through the spaces will know what I'm talking about. From that standpoint, by the way, books can never convey architectural experience.

The movement through the spaces and the way the light works are connected and central to the feeling and the concept. When they're really working, these spatial aspects are powerful; that's the music, that's the melody, that's the core. You have a concept, you have a conceptual drawing; that's the seed that drives the design. Then the design is measured in the experience, the success comes from the experiential nature. I'm very excited that the few people that have gotten into the Nelson-Atkins to drop down through that series of perspectives have been exhilarated. One reporter said, "Wow, it was like the space had been blown up into billowing sails from which light cascaded in." The building doesn't reveal that from the outside, which I really enjoy. I also enjoy the fact that held in this series of lenses that apparently sit in the grass is a whole exhilarating realm that has to be experienced, and in a way it's the secret of the place. You don't have to wear everything on your sleeve. Just because you have some swirling spaces inside doesn't mean you have to have swirling metal outside to tell you that they are there. I really like the muteness of the outside when it comes with the exhilaration of the spaces inside. That's the right proportion, with emphasis on the interior experience. I wouldn't want it the other way.

— Interview for *Architecture Spoken,* Rizzoli

48

2004

A new paradigm for cities is emerging in recent decades. Instead of architecture conceived as an autonomous object, instead of urbanism as an abstract planning discipline, and instead of landscape as a formal decorative surrounding for buildings, there is a new fusion of these disciplines. Emergent positive contributions: green roofs providing energy conservation, the atmospheric potential of building micro-climate landscape organizations, and the urbanistic focus on experiential phenomena from the pedestrian perspective, are all contributing factors in the development of this new "fusion."

During the previous architectural periods, from the neoclassical American architecture of the 1920s to the 1930s' European manifestos of modern architecture's rational language, architecture resulted in autonomous objects. During the problematic movement of the 1980s, postmodern eclecticism resulted in even larger object buildings, with pitched roofs, decorative historic applications, separated landscapes, and ultimately negative urban consequences, such as the impact of scattered decked blocks of parking garages.

At the beginning of the 21st century, with postmodernism and its reactionary movement of Deconstruction exhausted, a new compositional freedom emerged in architecture in conjunction with a continuing awareness of urbanism and environmental issues. The potential of fusing these disciplines is currently developing.

Our ongoing work at The Nelson-Atkins Museum of Art, like the Louisiana Museum in Denmark (from 1958), aspires to a fusion of architecture, landscape, and urbanism. From the very first design sketches we sought a visual link to the sculpture park and an actual merging with the landscape, inclusive of new sculpture park opportunities between the "lens" pavilions. Alternative to some of the other schemes from the 1999 competition, many of which included a mass blocking the north facade of the existing 1933 stone structures, our landscape of a reflective pool and the urbanism of a concealed parking garage is completed by an exemplary work of art by Walter De Maria titled *One Sun / 34 Moons*.

While the construction site is now raw and open, in several months it will be closed into the landscape and the ideals of a fusion Architecture, Landscape, and Urbanism will begin to be an experiential reality. With great honor and care we continue to work to preserve and restore the treasure-house of The Nelson Atkins Museum of Art and to complete a truly inspiring new addition that coincides with a new era in architecture for the 21st century.

—"Fusion: Architecture|Urbanism|Landscape"

2005

For me light is for space what sound is for music—the experience of architecture, the overlapping perspectives—it is the equivalent of spatial acoustics in light. If you have a piece of music, you have the score, you have the rhythm, you have some kind of polyphony, you have some kind of a structure, then there is sound that executes and brings it all to life. Otherwise, it is just an abstraction. The same applies to architecture: you have the spatial conception, the conceptual strategy, the integration of lenses in the landscape, the fusion of architecture and landscape and urbanism, but none of that is anything really alive until you infuse it with the light.

Spinoza said: "Good things are never easy. They are as difficult as they are rare." And this is a good thing, it wasn't easy, but it will be a rare thing. It is not just a new building; it is the contrast and complementary relationship between the great neoclassical building from 1933 and our new futuristic building. The balance gives you a thrust forward in time and a deep link to the historic past.

It is difficult to make an addition to a great 1933 building, to make something that really looks to the future, to integrate with the landscape, to do all these many things. And it is not small; it is 165,000 square feet. You could spend a day there; there are so many different perspectives. For me it has the potential to be the greatest thing I have yet made, because it began on an uncompromising, fundamental, conceptual strategy that was radical compared to all the other architects who approached the project, and it was supported by the trustees and the director of the Museum and not compromised in the process. To get all these things in place—it is very hard to get that to happen in your life. It is a very special chance, this building, and it plays a very special role in my work.

—KCUR Public Radio interview, Kansas City, Missouri

External simplicity/Inner immensity
The external austerity of the new building, "like shards of glass emerging from landscape," was, and is, fully intentional. I believe a building should always be much more about the interior experience than the exterior. The visitor will experience an external austerity followed by an inner immensity. It is the same strategy that Matisse used for his astonishing chapel at Vence, France, in 1952. It is the same philosophy informing our Chapel of St. Ignatius, Seattle, in 1997. I believe it is the correct strategy here; the original stone building stands free with integrity in the overall composition and the new lenses, or shards of glass, stand more minimally, forming garden courts for outdoor sculpture. The blank background of the glass planks is perfect for a foreground with a piece of sculpture.

The competition process was well run and courageous. The implication was to build on the north side of the existing building—a strategy that would cover this elevation forever and would not engage the potential of the overall landscape. We took the chance to depart from this mind-set and make an ideal scheme fused with the landscape, which would allow the original building to be restored with the integrity of its freestanding original proportions, rather than a lean-to or a new box against the original. We broke the new geometry down into five pieces merged with the (not yet there) landscape.

—Public forum, March 17, Kansas City, Missouri

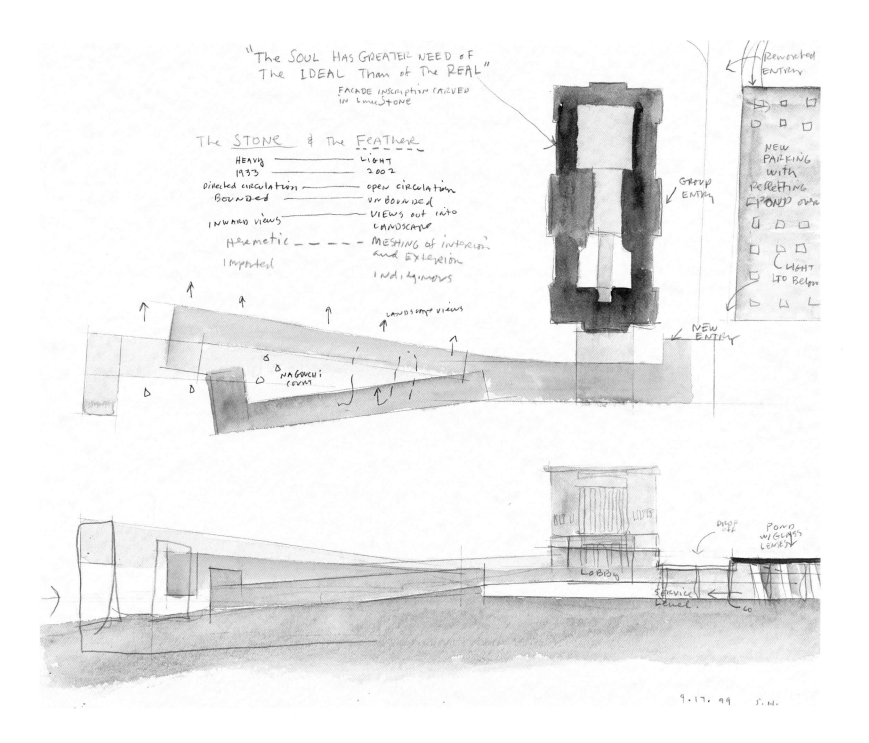

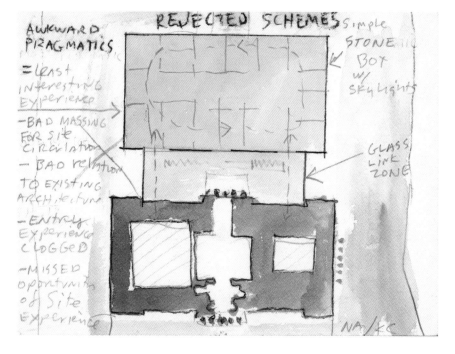

REJECTED SCHEMES

AWKWARD PRAGMATICS

= least interesting experience

—BAD MASSING FOR site circulation

— BAD relation TO EXISTING ARCHITECTURE

—ENTRY EXPERIENCE CLOGGED

—MISSED oportunity of Site experience

Simple STONE BOX w/ skylights

GLASS LINK ZONE

NA/KC

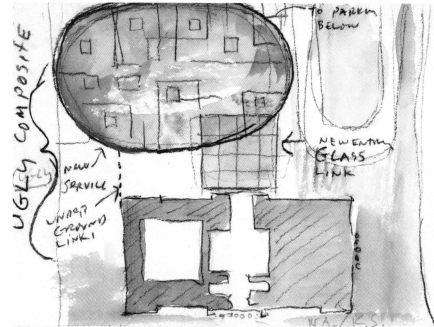

UGLY COMPOSITE

NEW SERVICE

unarp? GROUND LINK!

TO PARKING BELOW

NEW ENTRY GLASS LINK

NA/KC

52

Studies of rejected addition strategies.

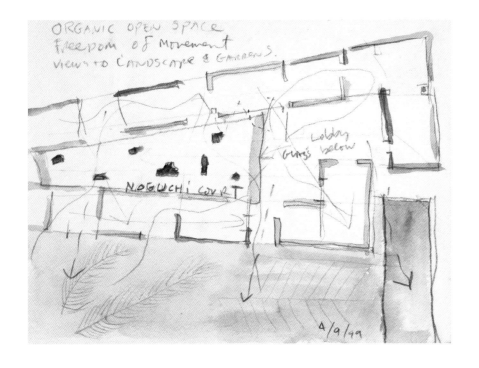

ORGANIC OPEN SPACE
FREEDOM OF MOVEMENT
VIEWS TO LANDSCAPE & GARDENS.

Lobby
glass below

NOGUCHI COURT

4/9/99

NELSON-ATKINS MUSEUM of ART KANSAS CITY 4/7/99 S.H

FOLDED
GOLDEN
WINGS
SCHEME B

SILVERY
KANSAS
Light

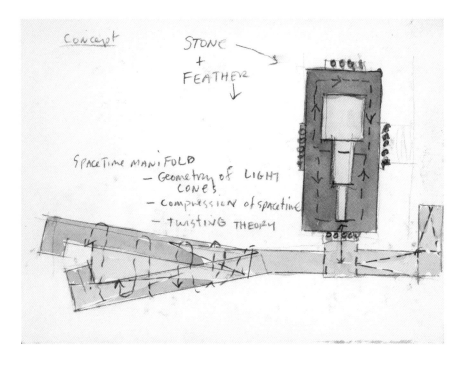

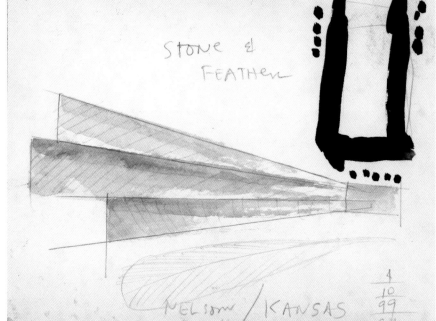

The Stone and the Feather.

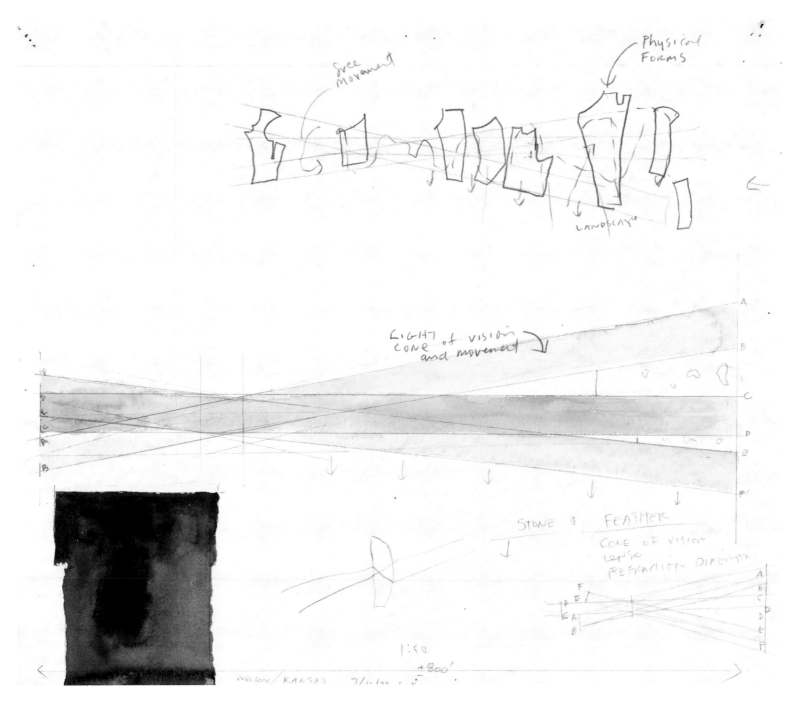

Study for lenses analogy to ways of seeing.

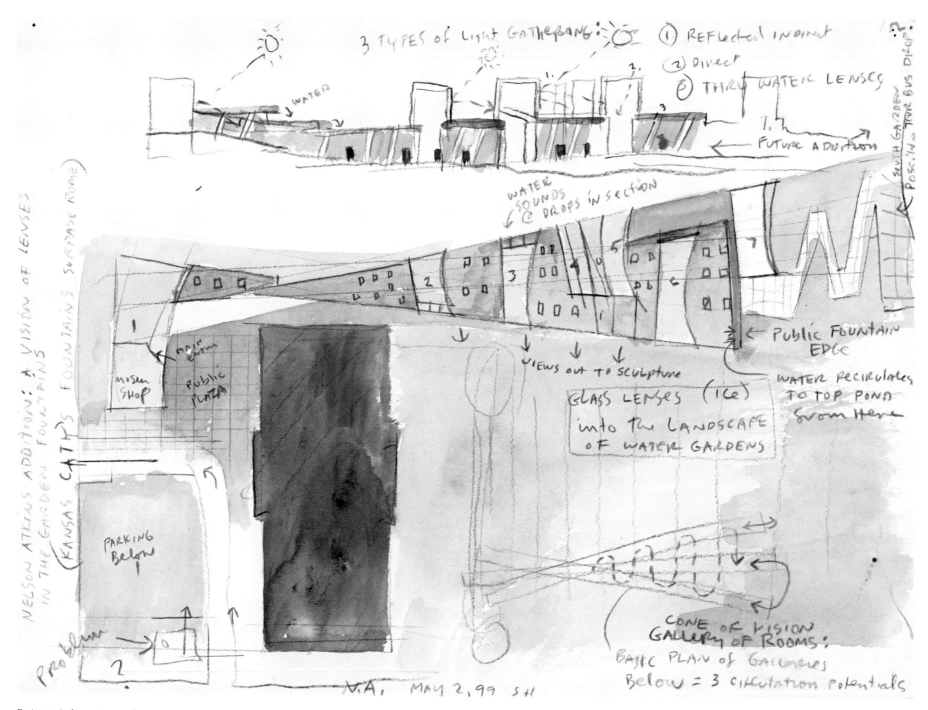

3 TYPES OF LIGHT GATHERING: ① REFLECTED INDIRECT
② DIRECT
③ THRU WATER LENSES

↓WATER

← FUTURE ADDITIONS

SOUTH GARDEN POSSIBLE TOUR BUS DROP.

WATER SOUNDS @ DROPS IN SECTION

PUBLIC FOUNTAIN EDGE

VIEWS OUT TO SCULPTURE

WATER RECIRCULATES TO TOP POND from Here

MUSEUM SHOP

PUBLIC PLAZA

main entry

NELSON ATKINS ADDITION: A VISION OF LENSES
IN THE GARDEN FOUNTAINS
(KANSAS CITY'S FOUNTAINS SURPASS ROME)

PARKING Below

PROBLEM

GLASS LENSES (ICE)
into the LANDSCAPE
OF WATER GARDENS

V.A. MAY 2, 99 SH

CONE OF VISION
GALLERY OF ROOMS:
BASIC PLAN OF GALLERIES
Below = 3 circulation potentials

56

Early study for water pools.

The Acropolis at Athens

"The Parthenon Meets the Plains" is a section heading of a book on the original Nelson-Atkins Museum, *High Ideals and Aspirations*. The most important building on the Acropolis at Athens, the Parthenon (6) was hidden from sight by walls of the sanctuary of Artemis Brauronia (4). It was necessary to pass through another propylon into an interior court to confront the splendor of the west facade.

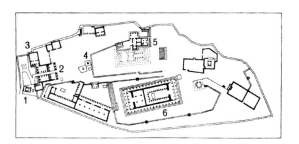

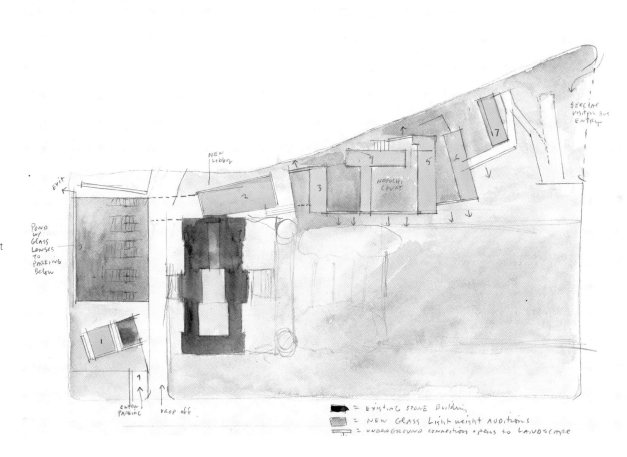

Comparison of shifting plans strategy at the Acropolis.

Lenses as icebergs floating in a lake.

Lenses as blocks of ice.

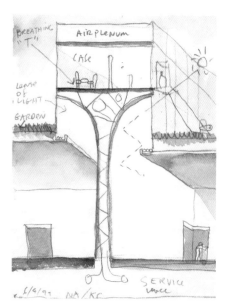

"Breathing-T" studies.

Parallax and light studies.

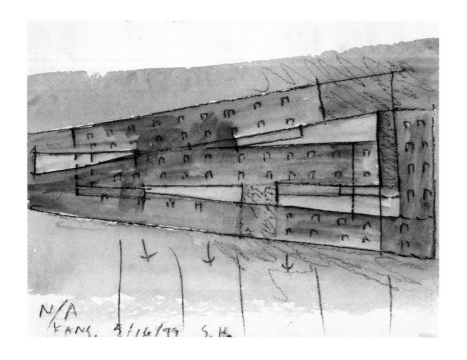

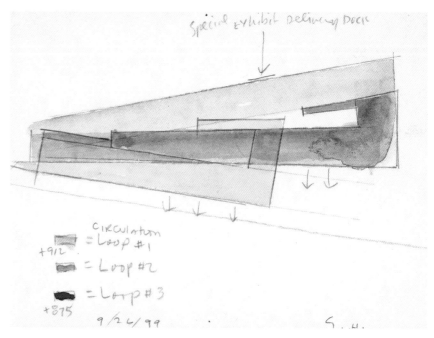

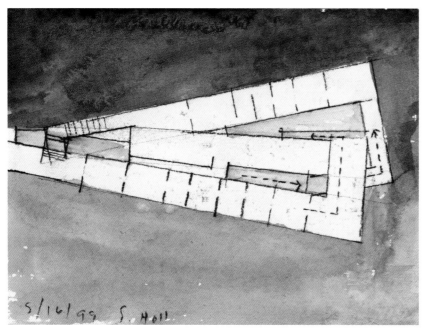

Studies for multiple routes.

MESHING OF INTERIOR-EXTERIOR
Nelson — KANSAS City S. Holl 4/17/9

Views to the existing sculpture park from the proposed addition.

The lenses bracket the sculpture park.

Study for Noguchi Sculpture Court with raw unfinished block of sculpture outside.

Study of first gallery looking back toward the entry.

African galleries study.

January 2007

Today we can finally see and experience this architecture the way it was imagined, in a view from the inside out. The fluttering Ts subtly mix the cool north light and the warm, yellow south light.

Structural glass "lenses," luminously bracketing the sculpture garden landscape, begin to glow from within at dusk. The dream of constructing in light reaches a comprehensive passion in this building. The interior of overlapping perspectives in subtle changing natural light is constructed from an exterior architecture of translucent prisms emerging from the ground—an architecture of sculpted bars of light and time.

One can really see that intensity in a billowing cloud-like spatial energy above the gallery floor. This light changes by the hour, changes by the day and by the season. It is as ephemeral as time. The spatial parallax experienced in moving through these galleries is also somehow related to time, whose passage is never in a straight line. Time is more mysterious, without a beginning, without an end, and without a final event. Likewise, these spaces turn and overlap with a cadence or rhythm, but, like time, without an absolutely defined direction.

A time relation is concretized with the new building opening to the Greco-Roman 1933 original museum architecture. The core of the Greek feeling about time was in cyclic return and the perfections in art and architecture relate to repetitive cycles. To the Greeks, a notion of continuous progress, of a time always new, was unheard of. Aristotle placed his "present" on a point in the revolving circle of time "after" the Trojan War. His time circle continued to rotate. "After" would eventually bring again the Trojan War. Unlike Buddhist time, Aristotle's eternal recurrence was only of type or species—not of the individual. The Greek cosmological conception of time depended on a specific vision of the universe, which was hierarchical and moving in a circle; it depended on the cyclical course of the stars.

Today, as we experience the open-ended geometry of the new architecture of The Nelson-Atkins Museum of Art, we experience its spatial energy personally, from the viewpoint of our eyes positioned in our moving bodies as they glide through the new spaces. It isn't just the idea of this architecture being "of its time" that is at stake here. It is a proposal aimed at the experience of moving through these spaces as an individual act. We personally open ourselves to art as a phenomenon of central importance to the collective and to the individual. Opening up to potential knowledge, opening up to reflect on and to become inspired by something greater than just "of our time," the hope is that we experience "we are our time."

PORTFOLIO

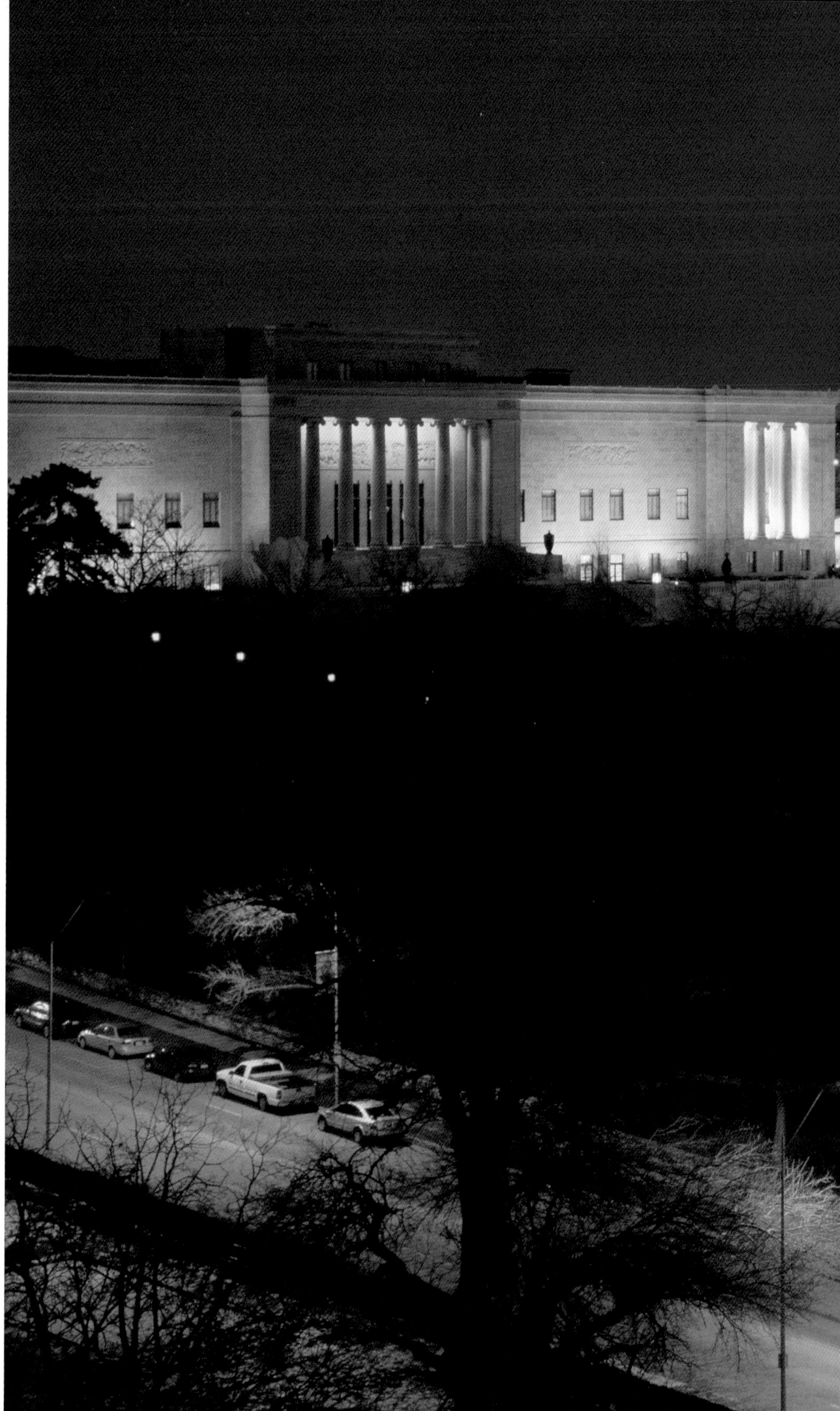

"The idea of complementary contrast drove our design for an addition to The Nelson-Atkins Museum of Art, a classical stone temple and surrounding landscape. The addition is not an object: we envisioned a new paradigm fusing landscape and architecture."

—Steven Holl

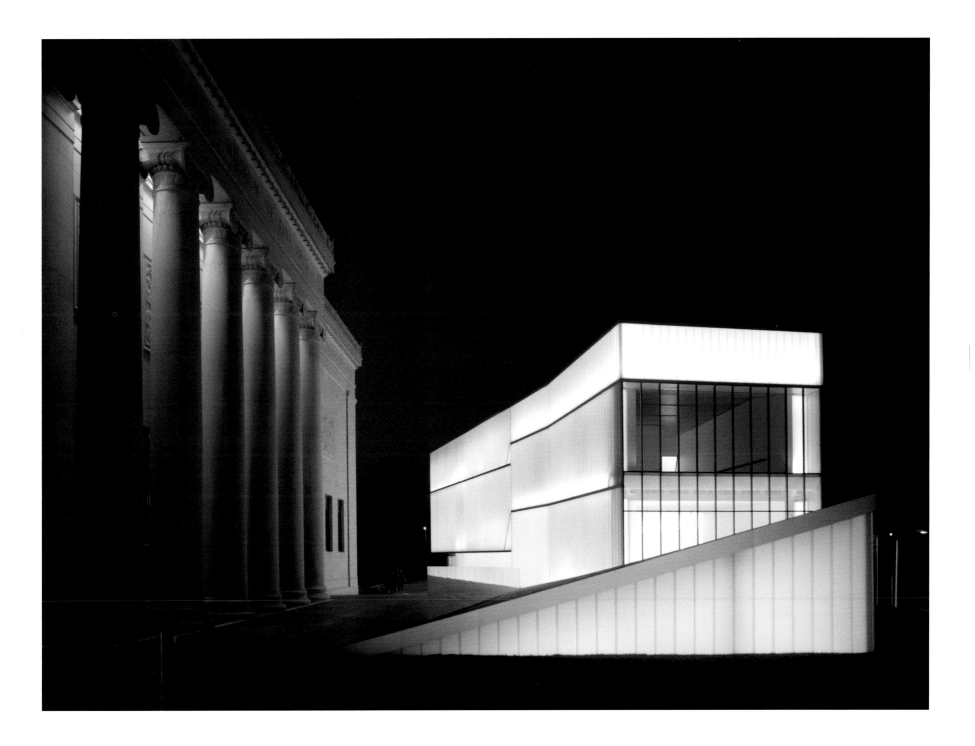

The lenses, whose new lightweight architecture of
glass contrasts with the stone Nelson-Atkins Building,
are scattered about the landscape.

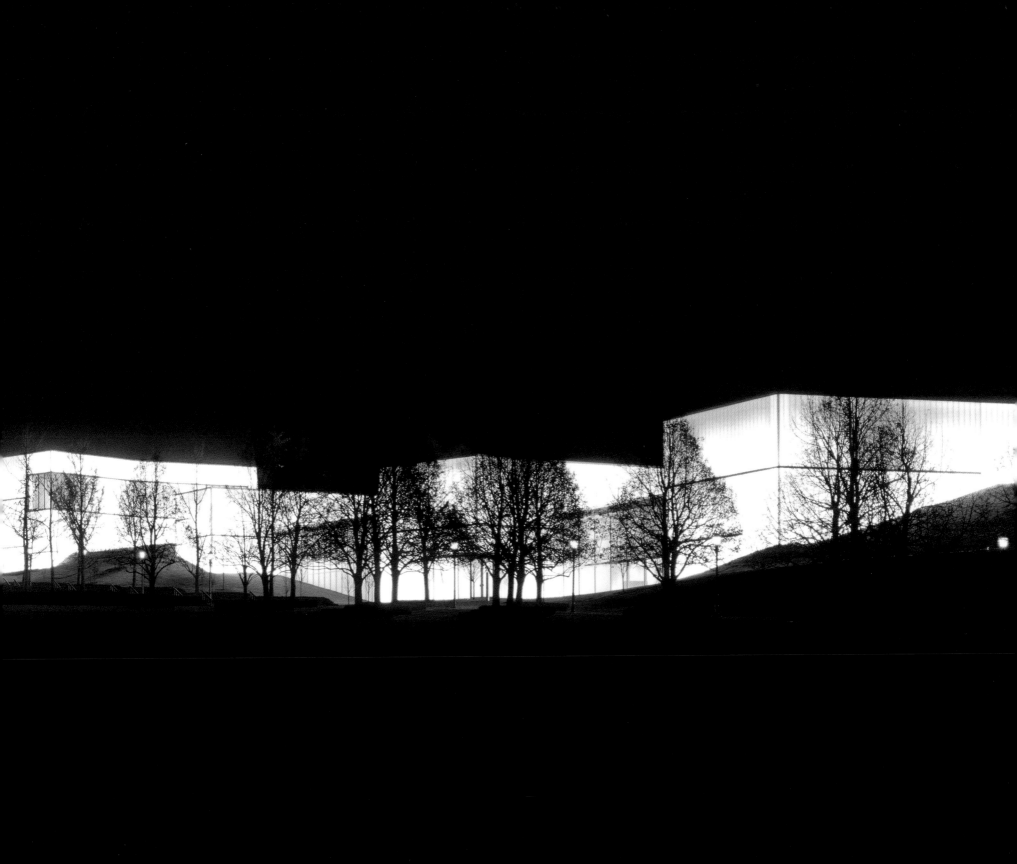

"The visual-spiritual experience of a museum visitor begins at the large reflecting pool of the north court. We collaborated with the artist Walter De Maria to realize his gold-leafed *One Sun / 34 Moons*. This large water body reflects the light by picking up the breeze in water ripples on a windy day, or capturing the reflection of clouds passing overhead on a day of scattered clouds and blue sky."

—Steven Holl

Seen from within the parking garage, the movements of wind and reflections of the sun on the pool above, transmitted by the round moon lenses, create dancing ripples on the garage floor.

"The external austerity of the new building, 'like shards of glass emerging from landscape,' was and is fully intentional: The visitor will experience an external austerity followed by an inner immensity."

—Steven Holl

The first of the five translucent lenses encloses a bright lobby, with café, art library, multipurpose room, and bookstore, inviting the public into the museum and encouraging movement via ramps toward the galleries as they progress downward into the garden.

The threaded movement between the light-gathering lenses of the Bloch Building weaves it into the landscape with a fluid dynamism based on a sensitive relationship to its context.

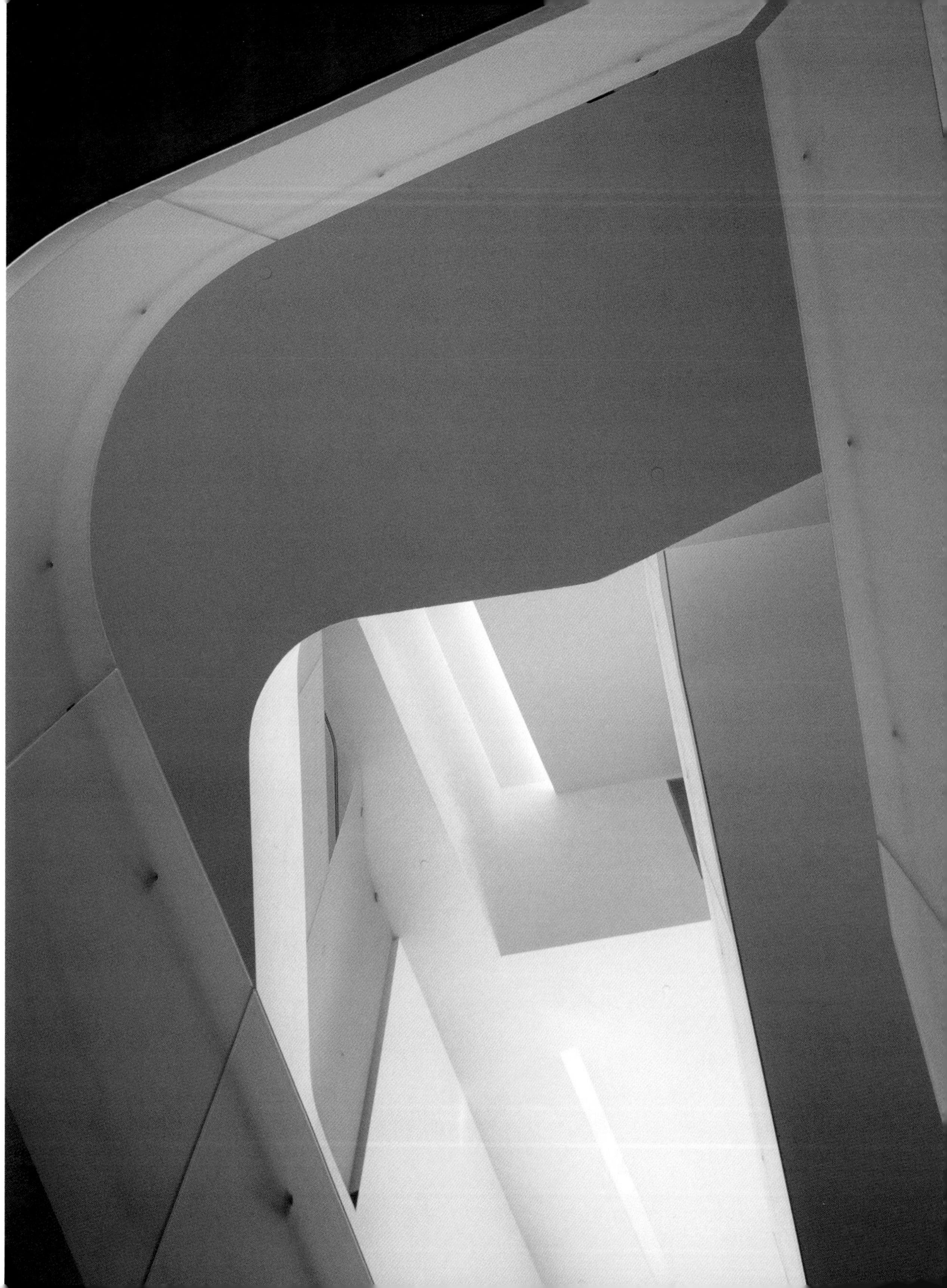

"For me light is for space what sound is for music . . .
If you have a piece of music, you have the score, you
have the rhythm, you have some kind of polyphony, you
have some kind of a structure, and then there is sound
that executes and brings it all to life. Otherwise it is just
an abstraction. The same applies to architecture: you have
the spatial conception, the conceptual strategy, the integration of lenses in the landscape, the fusion of architecture and landscape and urbanism; but none of that is really
alive until you infuse it with the light."

—Steven Holl

At night the glowing glass volume of the lobby draws visitors to events and activities. From the lobby, a new cross-axis connects through to the original building's grand spaces.

The collections are organized in a sequence of loops along a "gallery walk," allowing the visitor multiple options of engaging one or more collections without retracing a path. The continuum of spaces, linked by both aligned and offset openings for distant and shifting perspectives, carries the visitor through the diverse and differently scaled galleries.

William T. Kemper Galleries

All of the galleries are arranged on a continuous flowing level with occasional views into the landscape of the sculpture gardens. Circulation and viewing of collections and exhibitions merge as one looks from one level to another and from inside to outside. The back-and-forth "meander" path in the sculpture park above has its sinuous complement in the open flow of the gallery level below.

H&R Block Galleries

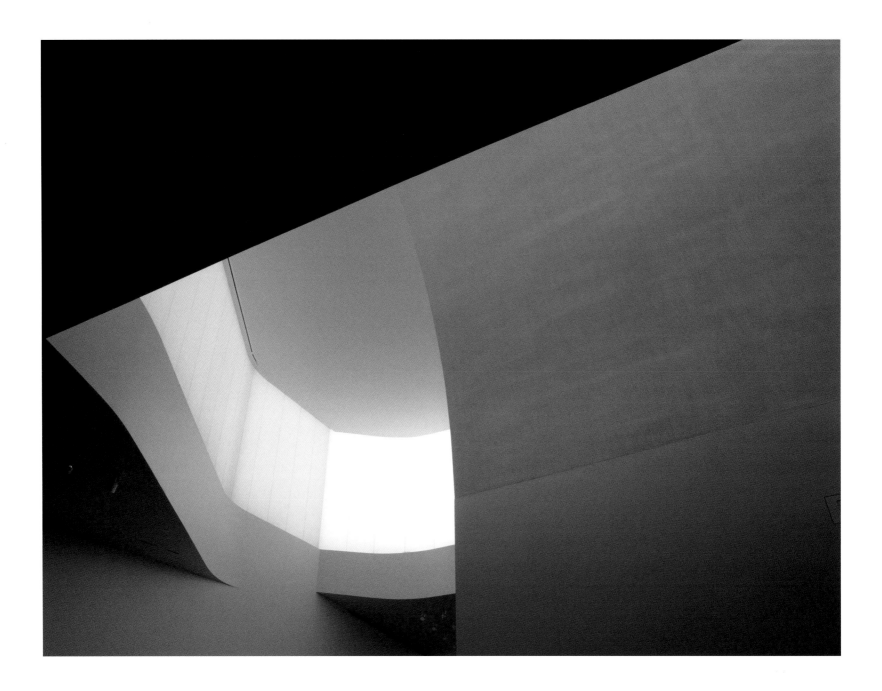

"The lenses celebrate the timeless fusion of art, architecture, and landscape. The new Noguchi Sculpture Court sets a binding, but natural, connection between the new building and the existing sculpture gardens."

— Steven Holl

"I really like the muteness of the outside
when it comes with the exhilaration of the
spaces inside. That's the right proportion,
with emphasis on the interior experience.
I wouldn't want it the other way."
                                    —Steven Holl

"The original stone building stands free
with integrity in the overall composition,
and the new lenses stand more minimally,
forming garden courts for outdoor sculpture.
The blank background of the white glass
foregrounds a work of sculpture."

—Steven Holl

173

DRAWINGS

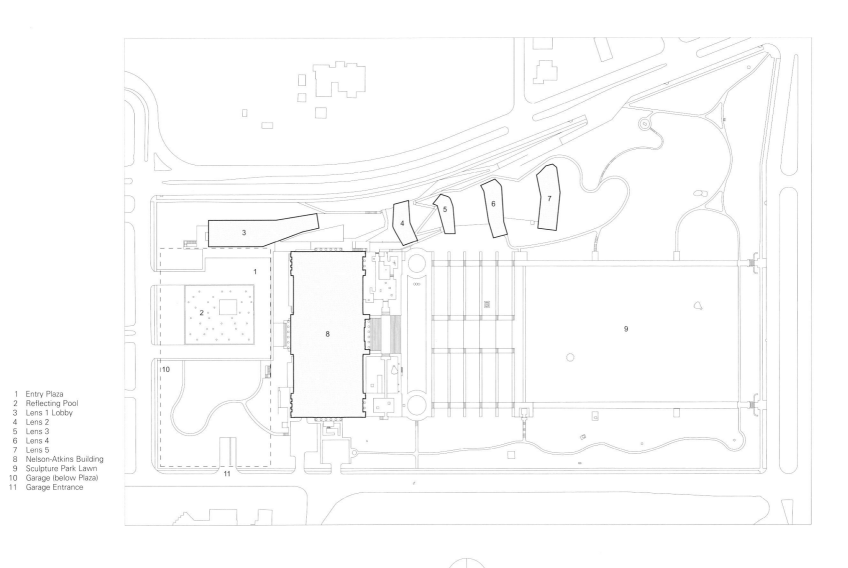

1 Entry Plaza
2 Reflecting Pool
3 Lens 1 Lobby
4 Lens 2
5 Lens 3
6 Lens 4
7 Lens 5
8 Nelson-Atkins Building
9 Sculpture Park Lawn
10 Garage (below Plaza)
11 Garage Entrance

0'   100'   300'   600'

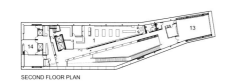

SECOND FLOOR PLAN

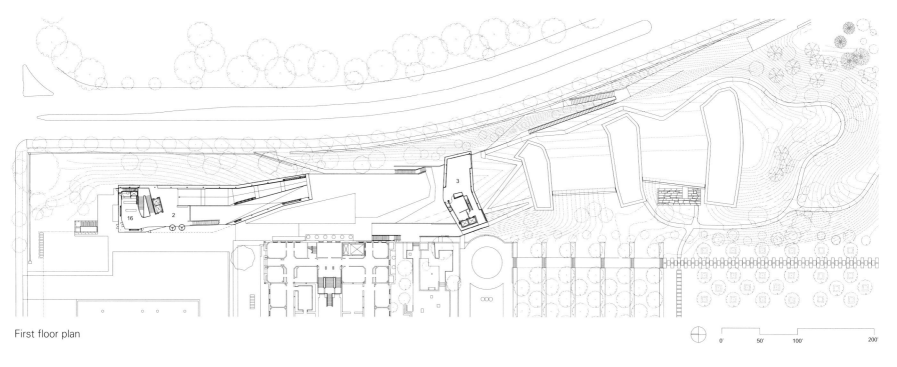

First floor plan

0'   50'   100'   200'

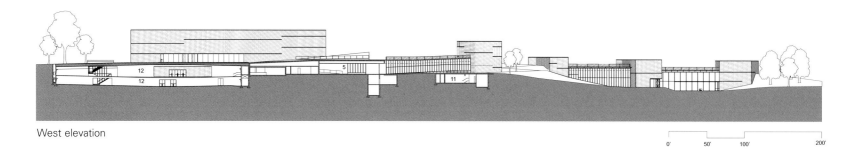

West elevation

0'   50'   100'   200'

1   Library
2   Upper Lobby
3   Event Room
4   Museum Store
5   Lower Lobby
6   Contemporary Art
7   Photography
8   African Art
9   Featured Exhibitions
10 Noguchi Court
11 Art Service Level
12 Parking
13 Multipurpose Room
14 Executive Offices
15 Auditorium
16 Café

Ground floor plan

0'   50'   100'   200'

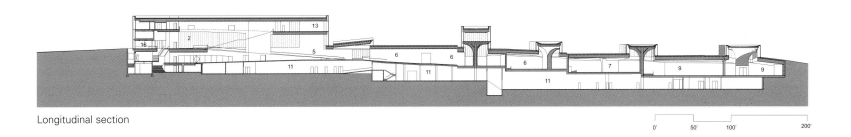

Longitudinal section

0'   50'   100'   200'

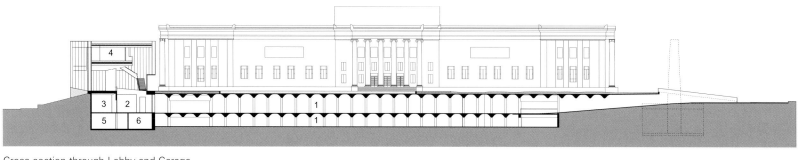

Cross section through Lobby and Garage

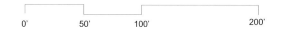

0'   50'   100'   200'

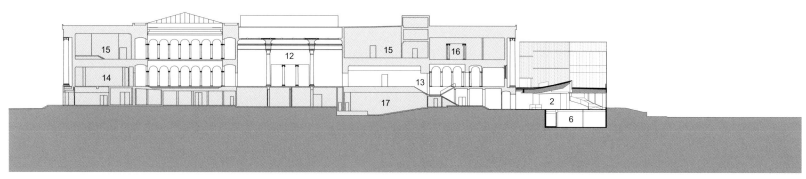

Cross section through Lower Lobby and original building through cross axis

0'   50'   100'   200'

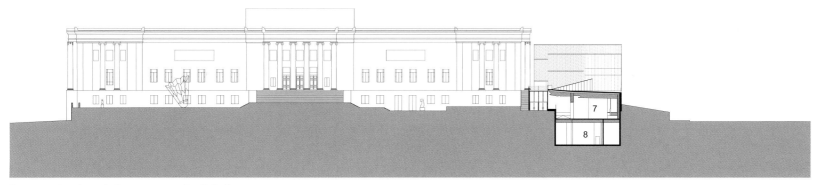

Cross section through Contemporary Art Galleries

1 Parking Garage
2 Lobby
3 Museum Store
4 Library
5 Stacks
6 Mechanical
7 Contemporary Art
8 Collection Storage
9 Noguchi Court
10 Special Exhibitions
11 Art Receiving
12 Original Building
13 New Opening & Stair
14 European Art
15 Asian Art
16 American Art
17 Auditorium

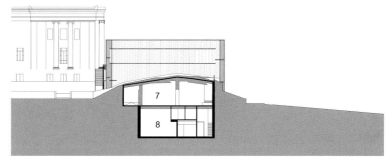

Cross section between Lenses 2 and 3

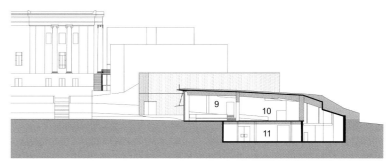

Cross section between Lenses 4 and 5

Building with Landscape and Light

Chris McVoy

An Expanded Field

The 1933 Nelson-Atkins Building embodies the traditional role of an art museum within society, an institution dedicated to collecting and preserving significant cultural artifacts. The symmetrical fronts, processional approach, elevated piano nobile, impervious stone perimeter, axial circulation, and hierarchical organization of rooms together monumentalize the visitor's encounter with the works of art. The charge given us to expand the original building offered the chance to fundamentally transform the museum toward a more open relationship with the city and develop a more subjective engagement with the art. During the competition briefing we realized that the expansive sculpture park, open to the public at all hours, could be the catalyst for a new museum architecture—one of landscape as much as building—joined to the exemplary original "Temple of Art."

The new Bloch Building, projecting into the urban landscape and traversing the sculpture park with several entry points, parallels the museum's expanding role as a cultural activity center integrated into the life of the city. The new building's spaces provide social platforms for the city's cultural programs and merge exhibition and circulation with multiple routes, allowing varying levels of experiencing the art. The gallery level opens to the sculpture park periodically as it steps down into the landscape; and the garden in turn continues up over the galleries, forming an indoor/outdoor museum porous to the surrounding cityscape.

An expanded field instead of an object, the continuous levels of the museum folded into the landscape and the five white glass "lenses" that emerge from them render the extent of the museum indeterminate from any single position. The lenses do not reveal the expanse of public space and galleries, which extends horizontally 840 feet into the landscape. The interior flow of circulation and gathering spaces lines the landscape and provides access to the entrance plaza, original building, and sculpture park. Visitors can experience the museum's exterior spaces, between the lenses and among the sculptures, at all hours.

The aim of fusing architecture and landscape opened up possibilities of shaping interior space in relation to landform rather than to building mass. The landscape is treated as a plane extended over the galleries, a "green" (planted) roof creased and pitched for continuity with the adjacent grades. The new building's floor levels rise and descend as the interior space flows down between bending ceiling planes, formed by the green roof above, and floors that cascade down into the sculpture garden. The landscape grade to each side follows in and out of sync with the floor levels, setting a varying relation between interior and landscape; the visitor moves down into the landscape only to unexpectedly arrive above it. In rhythms the building's section is developed as the plan—with bending space shifting in perspective as one moves through it—opening up as one turns a corner, converging and diverging along routes within the elongated body of the building. At five intervals the spatial flow turns upward within the lenses.

The 50,000-square-foot green roof minimizes the building's ecological footprint, providing a natural storm-water management system. The green roof's high insulation performance, and the large thermal mass of the below-grade construction reduce the energy required to maintain the strict environmental criteria of the Bloch Building's museum spaces. This construction, along with the retrofit of the original central plant, has resulted in an energy use for conditioning both buildings that is less than previously needed for the original building alone.

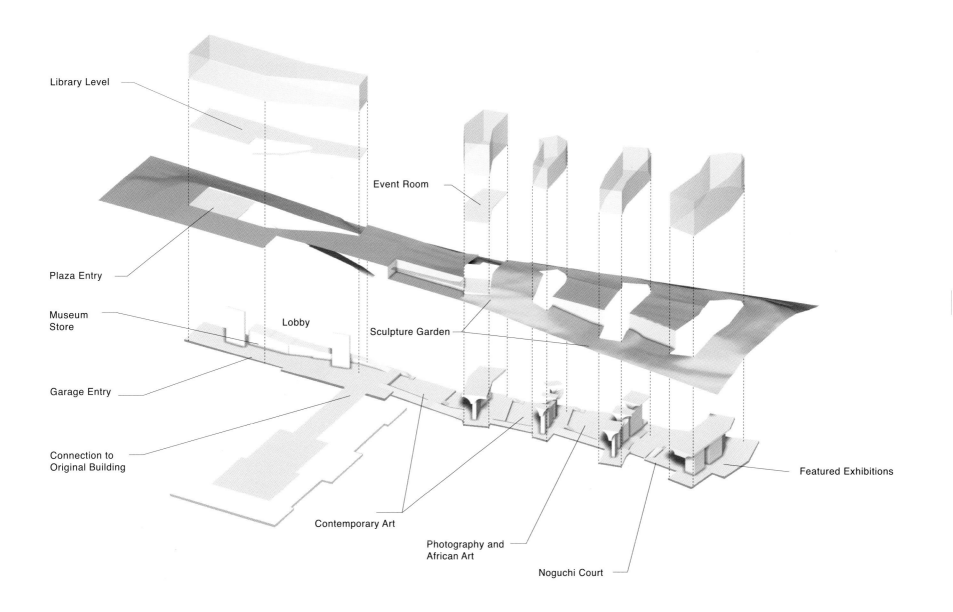

Library Level

Plaza Entry

Museum Store

Garage Entry

Connection to Original Building

Lobby

Event Room

Sculpture Garden

Contemporary Art

Photography and African Art

Noguchi Court

Featured Exhibitions

The elongated multi-level lobby connects the plaza and garage entries with garden access and a newly created cross axis through the original building's three major spaces. Rising 54 feet within the first lens, the lobby has ramped floors and open stairs linking three overlapping levels: the lower lobby with museum store and visitor services; the plaza lobby with café; and the second floor with multipurpose room and art reference library.

The collections are organized in sequential loops linked to a "Gallery Walk," a route that allows the visitor multiple options of engaging one or more collections without retracing a path. The continuum of gallery spaces, linked both by aligned openings for distant perspectives and by openings offset within spaces, carries the visitor through the diverse variously scaled galleries. The Contemporary, African, Photography, and Isamu Noguchi sculpture collections are linked but separate in a loose, nonhierarchical presentation. Particularity rather than repetition is employed, giving a unique spatial framework to each work of art and emphasizing differences in form, material, and thinking behind the works. With occasional views to the landscape and the original neoclassical building, the gently inclined Gallery Walk runs along the edge of the sculpture park, bending at each lens, and arrives at the Noguchi Court, designed specifically to hold the museum's significant collection of the artist's sculptures. The Noguchi Court doubles as a special-event space, and centers the Featured Exhibitions galleries around it with multiple entrances for up to four separate exhibition loops. The sculpture court opens along one wall to views of the sculpture park, extending the interior into the garden and fully merging the experience of art and landscape.

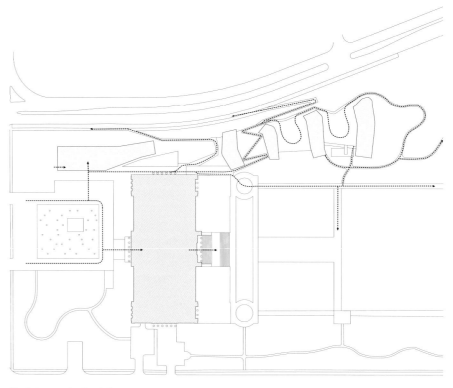

Sculpture park circulation

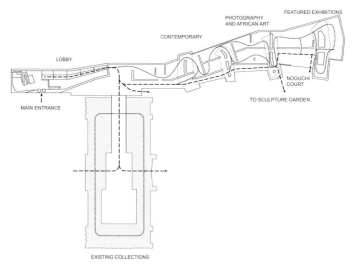

Gallery-level circulation

Lenses

The five white glass lenses create the Bloch Building's presence in the city. Volumes of light, they shape space between themselves, and in relation to the original building, creating intervals in the landscape. The lenses form interior space rising from below, where light plays down into the lobby and galleries.

Exhibiting both wave and particle qualities, light's infinite variation—its changing qualities across form and within space—is the primary material of the building. The lenses are instruments of light, gathering and diffusing natural light to the interior during the day and glowing in the sculpture park at night.

Each lens is made of one-meter-thick glass walls, with inner and outer layers separated by a pressurized air cavity. The glass layers are transformed by various processes—sandblasting, texturing, laminating, acid etching, iron reduction—reacting with light to create unpredictable phenomena: diffusion, diffraction, refraction, reflection, absorption.

The outer layer of the lens is formed of double interlocking glass planks with translucent capillary insulation between them. Each of the 16-inch-wide planks is extruded into a channel shape, then tempered, providing structural properties that allow it to self-span up to 18 feet, creating continuous translucent glass surfaces without vertical framing. The interlocking unit adapts to the bends and curves of the lens volumes, which are shaped to engage the visitor's movement between them.

Ferric oxide, which provides the greenish tint typical of glass, was removed from the glass for whiteness and to prevent coloring the lighting of the art. After experimenting with various treatments of the outer plank, we discovered that a combination of prismatic texture on the outer face of the glass with a sand-blasted surface on the inner face produced a silken sheen, which subtly refracts direct sunlight. Rather than the specular reflection characteristic of flat glass, the satin luster of the glass plank pulls the color of the surrounding sky or landscape across its surface. The lenses appear to trap light under certain conditions, and merge with the sky under others.

The lens wall's inner layer of low-iron, laminated, acid-etched glass, curving along with the outer layer, further diffuses the light to the interior, materializing it in the warm and cool glow of direct and indirect light changing on the surfaces as the sun moves through the sky. By the time the light has passed through the multiple layers of diffusion and diffraction caused by the glass treatments, it takes on an ethereal, mist-like quality that fills the volumes of the lenses.

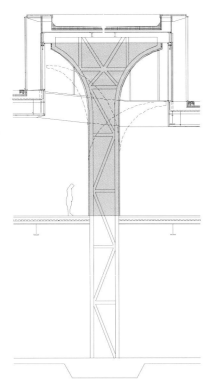

"T" section diagram Lens 3

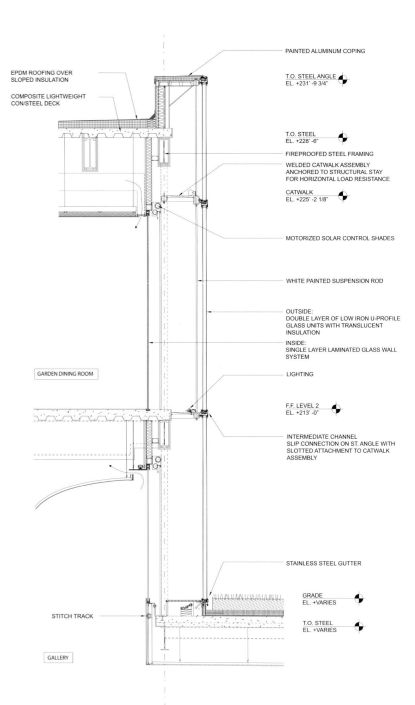

PAINTED ALUMINUM COPING

EPDM ROOFING OVER
SLOPED INSULATION

T.O. STEEL ANGLE
EL. +231'-9 3/4"

COMPOSITE LIGHTWEIGHT
CON/STEEL DECK

T.O. STEEL
EL. +228'-6"

FIREPROOFED STEEL FRAMING

WELDED CATWALK ASSEMBLY
ANCHORED TO STRUCTURAL STAY
FOR HORIZONTAL LOAD RESISTANCE

CATWALK
EL. +225'-2 1/8"

MOTORIZED SOLAR CONTROL SHADES

WHITE PAINTED SUSPENSION ROD

OUTSIDE:
DOUBLE LAYER OF LOW IRON U-PROFILE
GLASS UNITS WITH TRANSLUCENT
INSULATION

INSIDE:
SINGLE LAYER LAMINATED GLASS WALL
SYSTEM

GARDEN DINING ROOM

LIGHTING

F.F. LEVEL 2
EL. +213'-0"

INTERMEDIATE CHANNEL
SLIP CONNECTION ON ST. ANGLE WITH
SLOTTED ATTACHMENT TO CATWALK
ASSEMBLY

STAINLESS STEEL GUTTER

GRADE
EL. +VARIES

STITCH TRACK

T.O. STEEL
EL. +VARIES

GALLERY

The air cavity between the inner and outer glass layers is pressurized to buffer the interior art environment from exterior conditions for maximum energy efficiency. The computer-controlled shade screens within the cavities allow variable daylighting to meet conservation criteria for the full range of art media—including the possibility of near-blackout conditions for video works—and adjust for the differing seasonal light conditions. The complete lens assembly provides 18 percent visible light transmission for optimum natural light levels, while minimizing heat gain in the summer and harnessing solar gain and reducing heat loss in the winter. The multilayer lens assembly eliminates 99.88 percent of ultraviolet rays harmful to the art. The cavities also house structural elements, provide service access, and conceal the lens lighting—creating thick walls of glowing glass at night when viewed from inside and out.

T-Walls: Mixing North and South Light

At the core of each gallery lens is a thick wall containing the lens roof's steel structure and incorporating the air and service distribution. As it rises the wall curves outward in a T-shape, bringing the light down into the galleries along its cupped undersides.

The north exposure of the lens gathers the wide color variation and subtle intensity fluctuations of north light. Reflected off the atmosphere, north light registers the sky conditions—blue on a clear day, and often brighter on an overcast day as a result of its reflection from the clouds. The east, south, and west exposures of the lens diffuse the sun's warmer directional light, registering time through its changing intensity as it moves across the glass surfaces.

With their east-west orientation, the lens T-walls separate north and south light, then mix and modulate the two kinds of light through sculpted openings in the T-walls. Dubbed "fluttering Ts," these curved baffles and the tapered openings above them play the varying color and intensity of the light from differing exposures across their plaster surfaces. When flared to the north, the warm south light appears as a sliver within the cool diffusely lit cupped space of the T-wall. When flared to the south, warm south light crosses through the sculpted opening into the galleries on the north side of the T-walls.

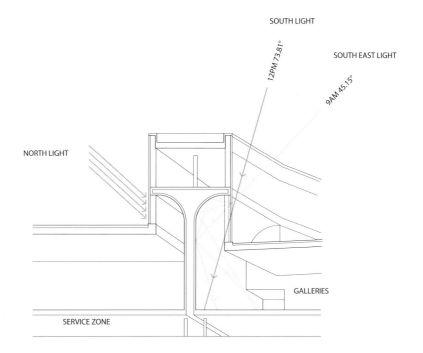

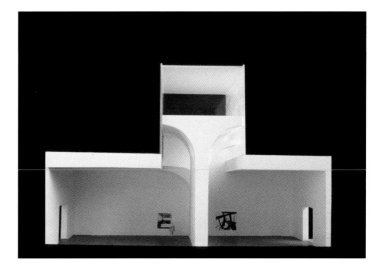

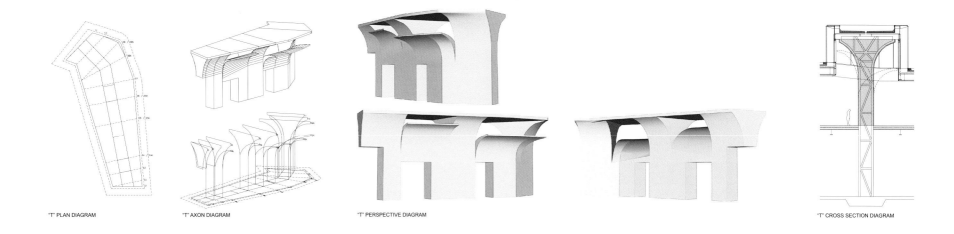

"T" PLAN DIAGRAM

"T" AXON DIAGRAM

"T" PERSPECTIVE DIAGRAM

"T" CROSS SECTION DIAGRAM

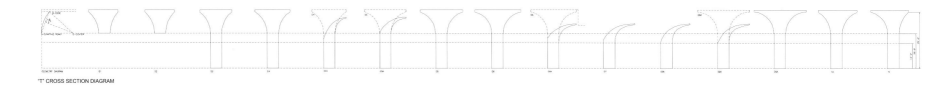

"T" CROSS SECTION DIAGRAM

Lens 3 T-wall

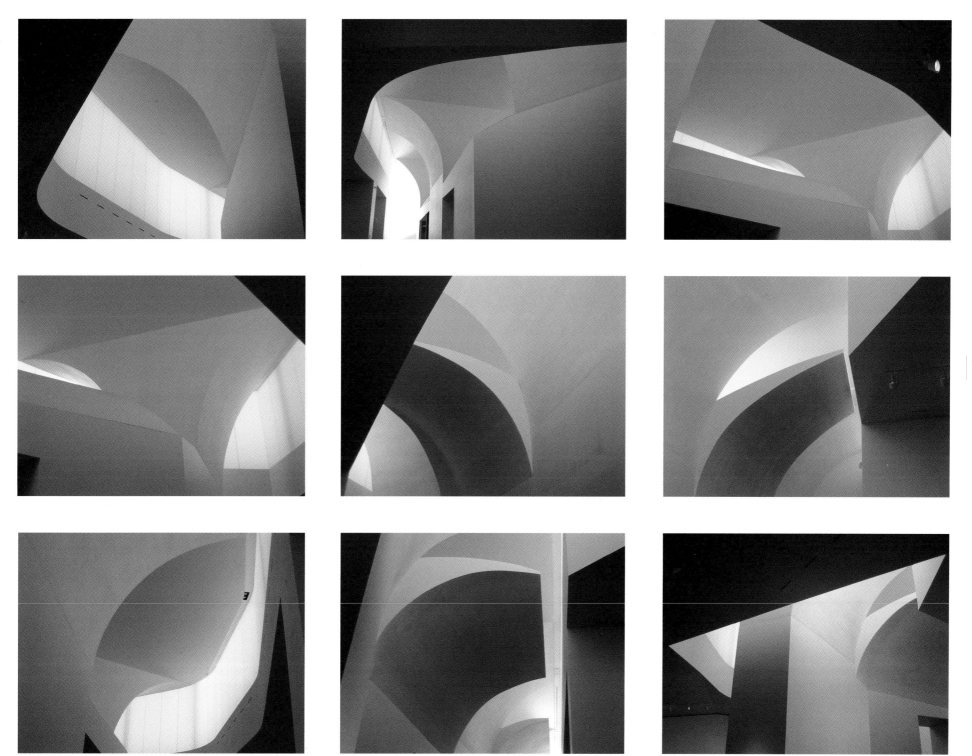

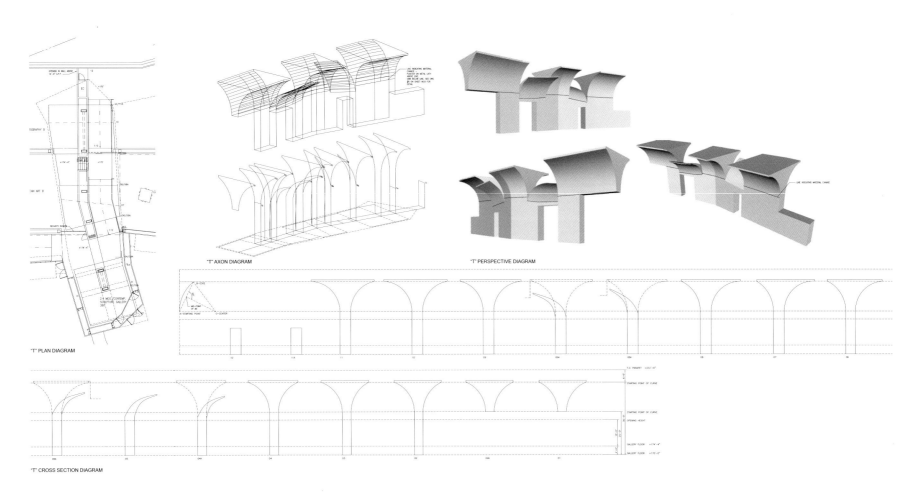

"T" PLAN DIAGRAM

"T" AXON DIAGRAM

"T" PERSPECTIVE DIAGRAM

"T" CROSS SECTION DIAGRAM

Lens 4 T-wall

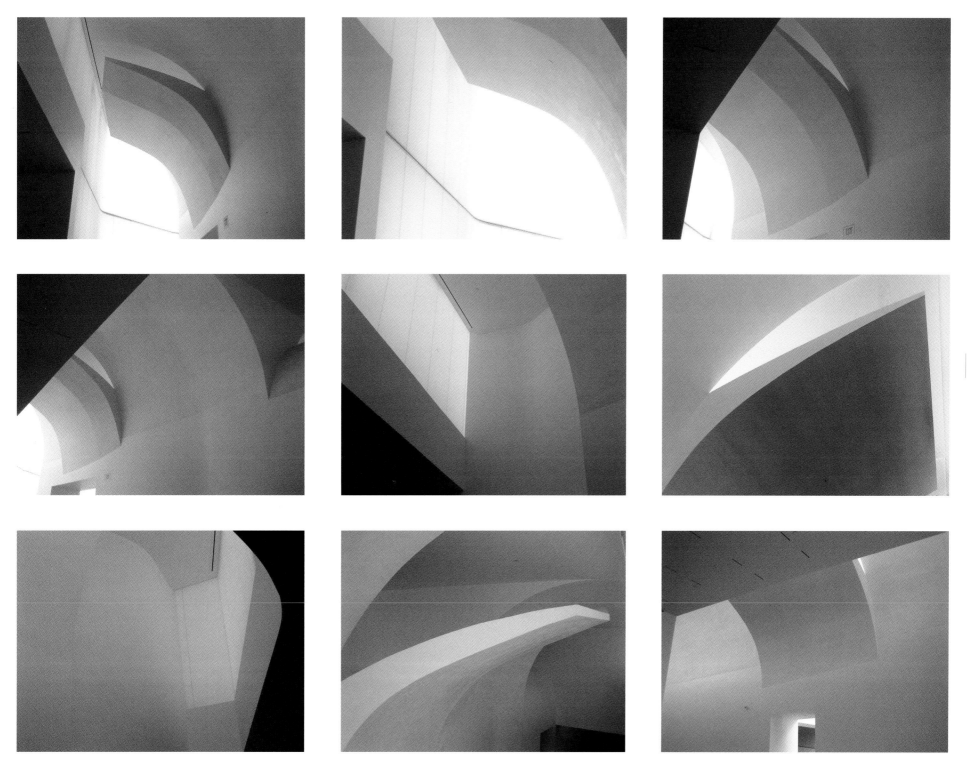

Gallery Light

The best conditions for viewing most types of art feature natural light with all its variation. Recent glass technologies that eliminate harmful ultraviolet rays offer new possibilities of bringing daylight into galleries. Typical gallery daylighting strategies employ various techniques to even out the light so that it falls within the narrow range acceptable for conservation requirements. Often all direct sunlight is blocked, and the ceiling becomes an unvarying surface of diffuse light in which natural light's changing qualities are suppressed.

We aimed instead to intensify and register the infinite variations of natural light through time within the space, to connect the viewer to the ambient exterior—the sun's position, the season, and atmospheric condition of the specific moment. To give the space and viewer dynamic light, while also satisfying the light levels set by conservation criteria, we established a datum 12 feet above the floor, below which the light levels meet the criteria and above which the light varies outside the range. The architectural volume is illuminated by natural light, and the art lighting is supplemented with electric light for focus and control. The pitched faceted ceiling of the galleries is carved out by the spatial volume of the lenses. As the walls extend above the art zone into the natural light of the lens, their form is organically sculpted to play in the light, to mix north and south light, and to emphasize the variations of color and intensity found in daylight.

While integrating the museum's cultural program into the everyday life of the city, the museum's architecture must nonetheless be removed from the environment of the everyday, with spaces of rarefied atmosphere for encountering the works of art. Art demands the viewer's sensitivity of perception. Around this engagement with the original artwork, architecture can concentrate on fundamental perceptual aspects of space, movement, materiality, and light, with the aim of a transcendent, united experience of art and architecture.

The Generations Capital Campaign

The Nelson-Atkins Museum of Art honors the following donors who made leadership gifts to the Generations Capital Campaign.

Principal Benefactors

Menefee D. and Mary Louise Harris Blackwell
Henry W. and Marion H. Bloch
Elizabeth Calvin Bonner
Ford Motor Company Fund
Donald J. and Adele M. Hall
Hall Family Foundation
Hallmark Cards, Incorporated
Shirley and Barnett Helzberg
Muriel McBrien Kauffman Foundation
Tinka and Harry McCray
Miller and Jeannette Nichols
Landon and Sarah Rowland
Estelle and Morton Sosland
Adelaide Cobb Ward

Major Benefactors

Anonymous (2)
Aquila, Inc.
Atterbury Family Foundation
The Baum Family in Honor of
    George K. Baum II
    G. Kenneth Baum
    Jonathan Baum
    Jessica Baum Pasmore
Jeanne McCray Beals
The Deramus Foundation
Charles A. and Barbara Duboc
J. E. Dunn Construction Company
Francis Family Foundation
The H & R Block Foundation
H & R Block, Inc.
Margaret Elizabeth Benton Humphrey
Frederic and Diana James
Kansas City Power & Light
The Kansas City Star
Julia Irene Kauffman

Julia Kauffman Donor Advised Fund
William T. Kemper Foundation–Commerce
    Bank, Trustee
Mabee Foundation
Barbara Hall Marshall and Family
Fred L. and Virginia U. Merrill
Celestin H. Meugniot
Missouri Arts Council Trust Fund
The Nerman Family
Oppenstein Brothers Foundation
The Hon. and Mrs. Charles H. Price II
The Victor E. and Caroline E. Schutte
    Foundations
Sosland Foundation
Rheta A. Sosland
Sprint Foundation
Richard J. Stern
Mr. David A. Stickelber
The Sunderland Foundation
The Courtney S. Turner Charitable Trust
Mr. and Mrs. R. Hugh "Pat" Uhlmann
Mr. and Mrs. James Crawford Ward Sr. and
    Irene Watkins Ward
Westar Energy

Benefactors

Lennie and Jerry Berkowitz
Butler Manufacturing Company Foundation
The Gary Dickinson Family Charitable
    Foundation
DST Systems, Inc.
Barbara and J. Peter Gattermeir
Mr. and Mrs. Harold J. Hudson Jr.
James M. Kemper Jr.
The L. Patton Kline Family
The Kosloff Foundation
Barbara James McGreevy
Judith Stern Randel
Mrs. Winston R. Tate

Major Patrons

American Century Companies
Andrews McMeel Universal Foundation
AT&T Foundation
Bank of America
Blackwell Sanders Peper Martin LLP
BMA / RBC Insurance 2003
Abe and Anna Bograd Memorial Trust
E. Kemper and Anna Curry Carter
    Community Memorial Trust, UMB
Mr. and Mrs. Thornton Cooke II
The Families of Peter and Kurt Gerson
Mr. and Mrs. Richard C. Green Jr.
Mrs. Robert C. Greenlease
Hale Family Foundation
Mrs. Alvin K. "Tillie" Heyle
Mr. and Mrs. Irvine O. Hockaday Jr.
Dennis and Carol Hudson
Mr. and Mrs. Laurence R. Jones Jr.
Ronald F. and Nancy J. Jones
John and Carol Kornitzer
Mr. and Mrs. Alan Reid Marsh
Merriman Foundation
Margaret S. Neal
Dr. R. Lyman and Sally J. Ott
Elaine Broudy Polsky
Richard J. Stern in honor of Eugene Happy
Mrs. Edwin H. Thompson
Waddell & Reed Financial, Inc.
Marc and Elizabeth Wilson

Patrons

Anonymous
Mr. and Mrs. George B. Ashby
Andrew L. Atterbury and Gwyn A. Prentice
Laurence E. Barreca
Mr. and Mrs. Paul D. Bartlett Jr.
Mr. and Mrs. Albert C. Bean Jr.
Dr. William Frank and Rebecca Culpepper
    Benson
Mr. Robert A. and Dr. Phyliss Bernstein
Delores DeWilde Bina and Robert F. Bina
Black & Veatch
Family of James H. and Rae Vile Block
Brace Charitable Trust–Bank of America,
    Trustee
The Breidenthal-Snyder Foundation
Mrs. Dean E. Broderson
Mrs. A. Keith Brodkin
Mr. and Mrs. Eugene D. Brown
Phillip S. and Peedee Brown
Mr. and Mrs. Richard P. Bruening
Burlington Northern Santa Fe Foundation
Stanley J. Bushman and Ann Canfield
Mrs. G. Guyton Carkener
Karen L. Christiansen
Michael and Jean Churchman
Barton J. and Phyllis Cohen
The Colom Family
Caroline Davis Cooke
Dr. Barry R. and Suzanne Taschetta Cooper
Bunni and Paul Copaken
Dr. and Mrs. James E. Crockett
Jerry and Vernon A. Davidson and Family
Mrs. Ilus W. Davis
Mr. and Mrs. Richard Manvel Davis
Jean Holmes Deacy
DeBruce Companies
Mrs. Robert A. Long Ellis
Mr. and Mrs. Brian D. Everist
Allen and Jeanie Fischer
Larry R. and Maureen V. Gamble
William and Christena Gautreaux

Architect Selection Committee

Donald J. Hall, *Chair*
Henry W. Bloch
Arthur S. Brisbane
John C. Gaunt, FAIA
Kathleen Collins
Vicki L. Noteis
Ada Louise Huxtable
J. Carter Brown
Marc F. Wilson

Advisers to the Architect Selection Committee:
Bill Lacy, FAIA, Special Adviser
Cary Goodman, FAIA, Professional Adviser
William Dunn Sr., Technical Adviser

Project Team

Program Manager: Lacy & Company,
 Kansas City, Missouri

Design Architect: Steven Holl Architects,
 New York, New York
Associate Architect, Architect of Record:
 BNIM Architects, Kansas City, Missouri

Lighting Design: Renfro Design Group, Inc.,
 New York, New York
Landscape Architect: Gould Evans Associates,
 Kansas City, Missouri
Mechanical, Electrical & Plumbing Engineer:
 Ove Arup & Partners, New York, New York
Associate Mechanical, Electrical & Plumbing
 Engineer: W. L. Cassell & Associates, Inc.,
 Kansas City, Missouri
Structural Engineer: Guy Nordenson &
 Associates, New York, New York
Associate Structural Engineer: Structural
 Engineering Associates, Kansas City,
 Missouri
Civil Engineer: SK Design Group, Inc.,
 Overland Park, Kansas

Glazing Consultant (Architect): R. A. Heintges
 Architects Consultants, New York,
 New York
Glazing Consultant (Owner): Heitmann &
 Associates, Inc., Chesterfield, Missouri
Glazing Consultant (Contractor): Gordon H.
 Smith Corp., New York, New York
Glazing Installer: Carter Glass Company, Inc.,
 Kansas City, Missouri
Acoustical Consultant: Acoustical Design
 Group, Inc., Mission, Kansas
Codes Consultant: FP&C Consultants, Inc.,
 Kansas City, Missouri
Commissioning Consultant: Facility Dynamics
 Engineering, Columbia, Maryland
Conservation Environment Consultant:
 Garrison/Lull Inc., Princeton Junction,
 New Jersey
Geotechnical Consultant: Terracon, Lenexa,
 Kansas
Information Technology Consultant: Affiliated
 Engineers, Inc., Madison, Wisconsin
Facility Program Consultant: E. Verner Johnson
 and Associates, Inc., Boston, Massachusetts
Security Consultant: C. H. Guernsey &
 Company/Layne Consultants International,
 Oklahoma City, Oklahoma/Parker, Colorado

Legal Counsel: Blackwell Sanders Peper Martin
 LLP, Kansas City, Missouri

General Contractor: J. E. Dunn Construction
 Company, Kansas City, Missouri

City of Kansas City, Missouri:
Donald Booth, Director of Codes
 Administration
Greg Franzen, Director of Inspections

Kansas City Parks and Recreation:
Mark McHenry, Director
Terry Dopson, Director (retired)

Book Team

Project Director
(The Nelson-Atkins
Museum of Art)
Deborah Emont Scott

Editorial Direction
(Prestel Publishing)
Christopher Lyon

Design
Bruce Campbell

Production Manager
Amanda Freymann

Editing
Stephanie Salomon

Research and Production
(Steven Holl Architects)
David van der Leer
and Ruth W. Lo